A History of
Professional Baseball
in
Asheville

A History of
Professional Baseball
in
Asheville

BILL BALLEW

WITHDRAWN

Charleston   London
History
PRESS

Published by The History Press
Charleston, SC 29403
www.historypress.net

Cover image: The Tourists had reason to celebrate after winning the Tri-State League crown in 1954 by thirteen games over second-place Knoxville. *Asheville Citizen-Times*.

First published 2007

Manufactured in the United Kingdom

ISBN 978.1.59629.176.8

Library of Congress Cataloging-in-Publication Data

Ballew, Bill, 1961-
A history of professional baseball in Asheville / Bill Ballew.
p. cm.
Includes bibliographical references.
ISBN 978-1-59629-176-8 (alk. paper)
1. Baseball--North Carolina--Asheville--History. I. Title.
GV863.N82B35 2007
796.357'640975688--dc22
2006034630

Notice: The information in this book is true and complete to the best of our knowledge. It is offered without guarantee on the part of the author or The History Press. The author and The History Press disclaim all liability in connection with the use of this book.

Contents

Acknowledgements

W hen all the contacts are compiled over the course of putting together a book, it never ceases to amaze how many people play a role in the process. Sean Henry and Mike Bauer of Palace Sports & Entertainment planted the seed, and Will Cleveland, formerly of The History Press, and my editor, Jenny Kaemmerlen, believed in the project. For the years I have picked their brains about the city's storied history, I thank Jim Baker, Mike Gore, Keith Jarrett and Bob Terrell. Ann Wright and Zoe Rhine at Pack Memorial Public Library were outstanding with their assistance once again. The National Baseball Hall of Fame, as always, showed why it's the best in the business, with Pat Kelly, Jenny McElroy and John Horne going above and beyond the call of duty.

Ron and Carolyn McKee deserve many thanks, from both me and the rest of the Asheville area for their twenty-six seasons of service to baseball. The old regime of Chris Smith, Larry Hawkins, David King and Joe Mikulik has kept the show going in addition to being good friends. Tony Farlow continues to shoot great pictures while keeping me laughing with his incredible sense of humor. Friends such as Kevin Flynn, Russell Hall and too many others to name play strong roles they may never realize.

Finally, thanks as always for their constant support go to my family—my wife, Hope, sons Brad and Bryce, parents Bill and Shirley, brother Sam, Brandy the beagle and mother-in-law, Faith O'Kelley.

Introduction

$\mathcal{T}$homas Wolfe loved baseball. Never were the author's feelings regarding the game more obvious than in a letter he penned to his longtime editor, Arthur Mann. Wrote Wolfe, "And is there anything that can tell more about an American summer than, say, the smell of the wooden bleachers in a small-town baseball park, that resinous, sultry, and exciting smell of the old dry wood."

Asheville's most acclaimed native writer was referring to his hometown in his note to Mann. Wolfe could have been referencing Oates Park, where as a teenager in 1915 he served as the occasional batboy for the Asheville Mountaineers prior to his departure for the University of North Carolina. Wolfe also may have had in mind McCormick Field, a place he visited after the wooden ballpark, with its left-field stands that declared "Asheville—The Playground Of America," opened in 1924.

Unwittingly, Wolfe began a lineage of sorts. Since Wolfe first fetched bats for the Mountaineers midway through the century's second decade, the job has been filled by a Who's Who of Asheville history. In 1961 Ron McKee, who served as the Tourists' general manager and part owner for more than a quarter century, handled the duties for the pennant-winning Tourists. McKee's replacement during a one-week family vacation at midseason was Roy Williams, the current head basketball coach of the North Carolina Tar Heels. Cal Ripken Jr. and brother Billy were batboys for three years in the 1970s when their father skippered the Asheville Orioles. Such modern-day standouts as Charles Thomas (Oakland A's) and Cameron Maybin (Detroit Tigers) discovered the protocol of a

Introduction

professional dugout in the same capacity during the late 1990s and early 2000s, respectively. The legacy will soon include Justin Jackson, the son of former Tourists outfielder Chuck Jackson.

The Asheville managerial duties also have served as a proving ground for skippers, with Billy Southworth, George "Sparky" Anderson and Cal Ripken Sr. honing their strategic skills in the Land of the Sky prior to advancing to the Major Leagues. Others, including Ray Hathaway and Joe Mikulik, emerged as local legends during their lengthy stints at the dugout helm of the Tourists.

As noteworthy as such efforts may be, those who play the game attract the crowds, and the Asheville cranks have had plenty of performances to applaud over the past century. Willie Stargell and Eddie Murray came through town early in their professional careers prior to earning induction into the Baseball Hall of Fame. Countless others have thrilled the masses, ranging from the antics of "Struttin' Bud" Shaney to Pat Putnam to Ian Stewart. Major Leaguers, too, have visited while partaking in exhibition contests—a roster that includes Ty Cobb, Lou Gehrig, Babe Ruth, Mel Ott, Hank Greenberg, Jackie Robinson, Duke Snider and Roy Campanella.

For a small town in which flat land is hard to find and everything is far removed from the bright lights of the big cities, Asheville's part in professional baseball is remarkable. What follows is the story of a mountain town that has seen its share of celebrities only the diamond game could offer.

First Inning

$\mathcal{H}$istory tells us that baseball began planting seeds throughout the South following the conclusion of the War Between the States. Union soldiers in prison camps introduced a version of the game known as "base ball" to their Confederate contemporaries, who then spread the pastime throughout the country after the conflict ended in 1865. A few Currier & Ives prints depict Union soldiers playing baseball in Southern prisons. The most famous one showed a game in Salisbury, North Carolina. Some observers claim another hails from a prison camp in Asheville, but local historians question the accuracy of such assertions.

Asheville was a fledgling town in the mid-1800s. The area was settled by the Davidson family in the early 1780s, and by 1840 the population had grown to six hundred. That total was modest by most accounts, yet there was no doubt the town was developing into a city that would serve as a hub for Western North Carolina. That fact became most obvious in 1862 during the Civil War when Asheville served as a training center for Confederate soldiers.

Various activities took root following the war's conclusion, and in 1866 the game made its first recorded debut in Asheville when a group of boys divided into two teams and toiled on the area's first baseball grounds, the Barn Field, also known as Smith's 118-Acre Tract. From that point baseball quickly replaced a similar game known as "town ball" as the sport of choice for local players. A handful of Civil War veterans went so far as to form an amateur baseball league consisting of several local towns, including Asheville, Canton and Waynesville and several teams consisting primarily of Native Americans.

A History of Professional Baseball in *Asheville*

Asheville's population remained fewer than twelve hundred in 1868. Bad roads and the lingering effects from the war's widespread destruction cut off Western North Carolina from the rest of the state. Significant growth did not take place until the railroad made it across the Eastern Continental Divide in 1880, bringing with it money and the first sightings of visitors. That same year Asheville installed the second electric streetcar system in the United States. The city quickly garnered a reputation as a tourist destination, particularly among the Victorian wealthy. Several lavish hotels and inns emerged, among them the Battery Park in 1889. Such attractions brought George W. Vanderbilt to town and led to his purchasing 125,000 acres of what he described as "the most beautiful place I have ever seen." Construction on Vanderbilt's 255-room mansion, which became the largest private residence in the United States, the Biltmore Estate, began in 1890 and was completed five years later.

By 1890, Asheville's population had grown to 10,240 people. As the city expanded like a sponge in water, so too did the recorded occurrences of baseball being played, even though the game was slow to develop since flat land came at such a premium in the mountains. Wendell Begley, a historian in the Black Mountain area, wrote about the game's increasing popularity in the late 1880s, when young men on the North Fork side of the Craggy Range met their contemporaries from the opposite side of the mountain in Reems Creek. According to Begley, the two sides climbed to the top of the range and met annually on the scenic mile-high meadows, then referred to as Craggy Flats and now known as Craggy Gardens, home to the world's largest natural rhododendron gardens. The game traditionally was followed by a social, with members of both mountain communities participating in the merrymaking. A similar event was held on July 4 at Carrier's Track in Asheville, which hosted a huge athletic celebration that included foot races, dog races and horse races. The 1893 meeting featured a two-inning exhibition game of baseball, consisting of teams known as "We-uns" and "You-uns."

The growing popularity of the sport led to the formation in 1897 of the Southeastern League, the circuit that served as Asheville's first foray into the national pastime. Donned in purple uniforms purchased by Frank Loughran, proprietor of the Hotel Berkeley, the Asheville Moonshiners hosted contests at Allandale Park, which had difficulty keeping some fly balls within its reaches to all fields. Located near the French Broad River, Allandale Park also bordered "Indian Territory," which reportedly featured teepees that housed the Native Americans who provided significant competition on the diamond during pickup games.

Manager John A. Jobe skippered the Moonshiners to an 11–10 record. The players received sixty dollars per three games played. An Asheville third baseman with the last name of Kleeman turned a triple play in a 9–7 Moonshiners victory at Knoxville. Another player, catcher Charlie Luskey, battled for his life briefly after being hit by a pitched ball.

By midseason the league was languishing in a variety of ways, particularly at the gate. The *Asheville Daily Citizen* wrote in its July 28, 1897 edition, "Has baseball partly lost interest for the town? The crowds ought to be twice as big as they are—and then some." The Moonshiners and the Chattanooga Blues were deemed too difficult and expensive for the loop's other teams to reach via trains, which resulted in the Southeastern League eliminating the two franchises before folding altogether on September 4. Feeling like soldiers without a war, the Moonshiners tried to form a Tri-State League, featuring teams from Concord, Swannanoa, Weaverville, Spartanburg, Columbia and Knoxville. After a few exhibition contests, financial difficulties prevented the circuit from materializing. A Western North Carolina League also failed to get off the ground shortly thereafter. In retrospect, it simply was not time for the professional game to blossom in the Land of the Sky.

A baseball game was played at Riverside Park as a fundraiser for Mission Hospital in 1905. At the far right is the Reverend W.T. Capers, who later was the bishop of south Texas. *Pack Memorial Public Library, Asheville, North Carolina, North Carolina Collection.*

A History of Professional Baseball in *Asheville*

The turn of the century saw Asheville become more vibrant, its reputation as a vacation Valhalla for travelers growing in the national media via laudatory articles and positive word-of-mouth advertising. The city's attractions also expanded beyond the scenic mountains and crisp air. Even though professional baseball did not reside in town, the game continued to spread throughout the region. Pickup performances on sandlots and organized leagues at the YMCA became more common. The sport also served as a staple of larger summer gatherings and even as a fundraising activity, such as a game played in approximately 1905 at Riverside Park to benefit Mission Hospital.

In 1904 Asheville joined Hendersonville, Brevard and Spartanburg in hosting a league of college players, beginning in early July. W.F. Randolph, the city's secretary of the Board of Trade and described in the *Asheville Daily Citizen* as a "baseball fiend," pushed the idea during a meeting at the Hotel Berkeley, noting the need for amusement for the city's visitors during the summer. The young men, it was decided, had to be "first class players who are anxious to come here to spend the summer and play ball." They worked for their board and incidental expenses for $7.50 per month.

Later that year, on September 9, 1904, the Cherokee team and the Madison County Mountaineers played baseball at Riverside Park. Much was made of the fact that seven members of the Cherokee club had played on the famous Carlisle University team. The *Asheville Daily Citizen* set the stage for an ominous affair, stating in a subhead that there were "Red Men After the Scalps of Pale Faces." The newspaper also promised, "The Indian team will wear beads and feathers during the game and Indians war-whoops will come forth at short intervals."

Although scalps were apparently spared in that 1904 contest, the local games became intense, and mountain rivalries developed into centerpieces of legend and lore, many of which would make the Hatfields and McCoys look like nursery school slap-fights. Such feelings dominated the Western North Carolina League, a four-team circuit in 1909 that consisted of Asheville, Hendersonville, Brevard and Canton. Slated to play a fifty-four-game schedule, beginning on July 12, the Asheville Red Birds played at Riverside Park, part of a large entertainment complex located on a small stretch of land that jutted out along the French Broad River at the bottom of Montford Avenue. A promotional piece described Riverside Park thus:

> *The popularity of this summer play ground is attested each warm season by daily throngs of recreators. Citizens and visitors alike mingle in the participation of its varied pleasures. Here are music, fireworks, moving pictures, swings, geological exhibits and baseball grounds. For those of*

Riverside Park was part of a large entertainment complex that served as the home to professional baseball for portions of the 1900s and 1910s. *Pack Memorial Public Library, Asheville, North Carolina, North Carolina Collection.*

quiet inclinations, shady walks for strolling and nature study along the shores of a beautiful lake with rippled surface, gay with happy boating parties. Many thousands of visitors from the torrid south, to avoid the summer's enervating heat, tarry at Asheville, enjoying comfort, rest and recreation at this delightful resort with its tranquil lake down by the swiftly flowing French Broad [Tahkeeostee] *River.*

The Red Birds posted a 22–20–2 record and were managed by Asheville native Stephen Andrew "Diamond" Lynch. By Labor Day, with the campaign nearing exhaustion, Asheville resided in third place, only a few games from the lead. Looking to win the city's first championship, Lynch allegedly acquired the services of players from a higher classification for the stretch drive. Peeved at Lynch's procedures, the other three teams voted to withdraw from the league, which forced the Red Birds to host some year-end exhibition games in order to pay the bills.

Despite Asheville's overall dissatisfaction with the Western North Carolina League and the transgressions associated with the circuit's demise, the Red Birds and their competitors received significant positive coverage in the local newspaper. At the conclusion of one story the *Daily Citizen* reported, "The game was wholesome, bang-up sport and every spectator got a large money's worth." Perhaps the most notable effort from the season was the Asheville team's "moonlight" game on August 23 against the Cherokee independent team, with the help of fifty arc lights temporarily erected at Riverside Park.

Baseball was back in 1910, with the Asheville Moonshiners facing clubs from Rome, Georgia; Gadsden, Alabama; and three Tennessee towns—Knoxville, Morristown and Johnson City—in the Southeastern League. Dave Gaston managed the Asheville nine and Candler's Jim Gudger was among the players that helped the team place fourth in the league with a 44–41 record. A year later, in 1911, the league showed Rome and Gadsden the door and added two more Tennessee entries—Bristol and Cleveland—to the circuit, renamed the Appalachian League. The changes enabled the Moonshiners to move up to third place with a 53–45 record, thanks in part to B.B. Woodward's league-leading 11 home runs.

Yet things were not rosy on the baseball front in Asheville. The Moonshiners were the loop's poorest attraction on the road and averaged only four hundred fans per game to their home contests at Riverside Park in 1911. The Appalachian League as a whole was a financial flop, and city officials looked for alternatives. Asheville received an opportunity to move to the North Carolina League, a shift supported by those on numerous fronts. For reasons never explained, the team opted to give the Appalachian League another chance and returned to the circuit in 1912.

l, J. R. Oates, Dir.; 2, Duckett, Sec.; 3, Frye; 4, Doak; 5, Noojin; 6, Stafford; 7, McKeithan; 8, Griffin; 9, Holland; 10, Barbare; 11, Milliman; 12, 3umb; 13, Corbett; 14, Wilbar; 15, Watson; 16, Stouch, Mgr.   Pelton, Photo.
ASHEVILLE TEAM—NORTH CAROLINA LEAGUE.

The 1912 season was the Asheville Moonshiners' final year in the Appalachian League. Asheville, pictured here in *Spalding's Official Base Ball Guide* from 1913, went 47–58. *Author's collection.*

After a fifth-place finish with a 47–58 record in the Appalachian League in 1912, Asheville baseball started to mirror the city's progress of the same period. The Land of the Sky attracted the well-to-do like ants to a sugar cube with the building of the Langren Hotel in 1912, the 510-room Grove Park Inn in 1913 and the Kenilworth Inn in 1918. Presidents, actors and authors arrived at the magnificent facilities on a regular basis, all in search of some rest and relaxation as well as the healing powers of the clean mountain air.

Baseball fever took hold of Asheville shortly thereafter. Beginning in the early 1910s, the *Citizen* showed play-by-play results of the World Series on boards outside of the newspaper's downtown offices. Using the business's leased wire, connected with the Associated Press box at the ballpark and extra telephone service for the games, the newspaper revealed results within a minute of the action on the distant field. Estimates had more than two thousand locals following the events of the Fall Classic well into the middle of the 1920s, when radio became more widespread.

The Asheville baseball team made three significant changes during this period. The Mountaineers relocated to the Class D North Carolina League in 1913. Contributing to the team's financial woes, the club also moved from Riverside Park, where nearby Riverside Lake swallowed baseballs like bait, to Oates Park. The new baseball field was named for J. Rush Oates, who was named director of the team in 1913 and described in the *Citizen* as a man who had "always taken an active part in all movements looking to better baseball in Asheville."

Located in the triangle bounded by McDowell, Choctaw and Southside Streets, easily within reach on the city's streetcar system, Oates Park seated twelve hundred fans. The field's layout included a cavernous right-center field, and while the dimensions to left and straightaway center were not particularly long, a high fence prevented most big flies from leaving the yard. A scoreboard with a large imitation coffee urn and a wooden cutout advertising Bull Durham tobacco begged for attention on the center field wall.

Competing against teams from Winston-Salem, Durham, Raleigh, Charlotte and Greensboro, the loop's lone entry from the western half of the state posted a respectable 58–55 mark. Harry Watson made history by throwing the first no-hitter for an Asheville team, accomplishing the feat on August 6, 1913, in a 3–0 triumph over the Winston-Salem Twins. Watson's gem was one of four no-hitters thrown in the minor leagues on that date.

Earlier that spring, Ty Cobb, a fiery outfielder and one of the premier players of all time, was in the midst of a contract dispute with the Detroit Tigers. Instead of twiddling his thumbs during the stalemate, Cobb put

A History of Professional Baseball in *Asheville*

Ty Cobb visited Asheville for exhibition games in 1913 and 1924. Cobb hit a home run in the first official game at McCormick Field in 1924. *National Baseball Hall of Fame Library, Cooperstown, New York.*

together a team of "baseball artists" that traveled to Southern cities during the early spring to play exhibition games. Cobb's crew arrived in Asheville on April 8, 1913, to meet manager Tommy Stouch's Mountaineers at Oates Park. The visitors arrived two players shy of a team after they missed the train, forcing Cobb to recruit a pair of locals.

Cobb, who also earned some cash aside from his Detroit contract by participating in various onstage performances, stayed with his team at the Langren Hotel. A mob descended upon the lobby when the future Hall of Famer arrived. According to the *Asheville Gazette-News*, "There were so many who were desirous of shaking his hand that it was hard for him to get away for dinner. He received them all in the bashful manner that was characteristic of his previous visit here as the 'star' in *The College Widow*."

A week earlier, on April 1–2, 1913, the Mountaineers christened Oates Park when Tommy Stouch's team faced the Philadelphia Athletics, managed by Cornelius McGillicuddy, better known as Connie Mack. The Athletics were one of the Major Leagues' premier teams and went on to win the World Series over the New York Giants later that fall. Among the A's who made the trip for the two-game exhibition contests was future Hall of Fame pitcher Chief Bender, who went 21–10 that year for the Philadelphia club.

Known on occasion in the local newspapers as "Tourists" for the first time, the Asheville nine struggled to remain afloat financially in 1914. The city also received a visit from the rookies of the New York Giants on April 6, 1914. Jim Thorpe, just two years removed from winning gold in the Stockholm Olympics, played for the Giants and swatted a three-run homer during the exhibition game. The Asheville team's struggles extended beyond the financial balance sheet, with the club finishing last in the North Carolina State League with a 43–73 record.

1, Ostermeyer; 2, Brittain; 3, Kelly; 4, Frye; 5, A. Watson; 6, Bumb; 7. H. Watson; 8, Corbett, Mgr.; 9, Lowe; 10, Clapp; 11, Schuyler; 12, Fortune; 13, Howard; 14, Ferris. Barnhill, Photo.

ASHEVILLE TEAM—NORTH CAROLINA LEAGUE.

The Asheville Mountaineers, pictured here in *Spalding's Official Base Ball Guide*, moved to the North Carolina State League and from Riverside Park to Oates Park in 1913. *Author's collection.*

A History of Professional Baseball in *Asheville*

Their fortunes were reversed a year later when the team went from worst to first by winning the North Carolina State League title with a 74–46 record. The North Carolina League for the first time went with a split-season format after Asheville opened the year with 39 wins in its first 60 games. The Tourists, however, killed any hope of a playoff by winning the second half as well with a 35–25 mark. On April 24, 1915, pitcher Gary Fortune fanned 21 batters and allowed only 8 hits in a 12-inning contest, yet lost to Winston-Salem, 5–4. Fortune, who split 10 decisions with Asheville the previous season, went 22–10 in 1915 and limited opponents to 241 hits in 309 innings. The High Point native pitched in the Major Leagues with Philadelphia and Boston before returning to Asheville as a thirty-one-year-old in 1926, when he won 5 of 7 decisions with a 3.33 ERA.

Fortune and his fellow Asheville hurlers, headed by 27-game winner Doc Ferris, received offensive assistance from Jimmy Hickman, who was sent to the team by the Brooklyn Robins and led the North Carolina State League in 1915 with 95 runs scored, 127 hits and 14 home runs. Teammate Dallas Bradshaw also contributed by tying Hickman for the league lead in hits. Their bats helped guide the team to the playoffs, where Asheville met the Rocky Mount Carolinians, winners of the Virginia League, in the Virginia–North Carolina Series, won by the Tourists 4 games to 2.

Jimmy Hickman returned to Asheville in 1916 and led the league with a .350 batting average. On August 17, 1916, the outfielder batted 9 times during a doubleheader and recorded a home run, double and 6 singles while stealing 4 bases to help sweep the Greensboro Hillbillies.

Another notable member of the 1916 club was catcher Earle Mack, the son of Philadelphia A's skipper Connie Mack, who attended a handful of games in Asheville that year to scout his son and other potential Major Leaguers. One of those visits occurred on April 5–6 when the Athletics faced a team known as the Paramounts. The A's were scheduled to meet the Tourists, but a ruling of baseball's National Commission said the club could not organize until April 11. Since most of the Asheville players were already in town in preparation for the season, the team was composed primarily of Tourists.

The visitors took the first contest in a tightly played 3–2 decision until darkness forced an early curtain after eight innings, but not before a hurler named Bland, a star cadet athlete at nearby Bingham Military Academy, struck out future Hall of Famer Napoleon Lajoie. More than a thousand fans crammed into Oates Park, with the *Asheville Citizen* noting, "among whom were a large number of the fair sex." All of the receipts from the game were earmarked "to benefit the training fund of the Asheville Baseball Club."

Highlighting the two games was a "monster banquet" at the Langren Hotel. Just prior to the start of the fourth inning, Asheville team president L.L. Jenkins took the field in a Tourists' uniform and announced plans for the evening's gala, suggesting the fans arrive early in order to avoid the rush. Connie Mack, meanwhile, was a frequent visitor to the city. In later years, he visited his daughter's home in the Beaver Lake section on several occasions during her lengthy illness that led to her death in Asheville.

Asheville's 1915 team in the North Carolina State League swept both halves of the season. The club was also known as the Tourists for the first time in franchise history. *Bob Terrell collection.*

A History of Professional Baseball in *Asheville*

Connie Mack, who managed the Philadelphia A's for fifty years, is shown here with his sons, including Earle pictured on his right, who caught five games for Philadelphia from 1910 to 1914 and was the Tourists' receiver in 1916. *National Baseball Hall of Fame Library, Cooperstown, New York.*

The flood of 1916, which hit the city on July 16, washed away Riverside Park and forced the Asheville club to embark on a twenty-game road trip. With the waters wiping out numerous homes and a significant portion of the Southern railroad east of Asheville, the team did not play anywhere for an extended stretch until the tracks were reconnected along the Swannanoa River. Much like an old-timer's tale of trudging five miles through a foot of snow to school every day, a story was repeated for years that had the baseball team walking upwards of twenty miles to Ridgecrest with their uniforms and equipment slung over shoulders in order to catch a train to meet their eastern rivals. The Tourists did fall to fourth place with a 58–54 record, yet still managed to qualify for the playoffs by winning the first-half title before losing four straight to the second-half champs, the Charlotte Hornets.

Managing the team during this successful stretch was Jack Corbett, who took over the Asheville club during the 1914 season. During the first two decades of the twentieth century, managers as well as umpires found their lives in constant peril. The sound of fans yelling, "Kill the umpire!" was not only commonplace, but was also nearly taken literally on occasion. Skippers were harassed and doubted, their strategy a constant lightning rod for criticism. Few finished a full season.

Turnover at the dugout helm prevailed in Asheville. While Dave Gaston survived the entire season in 1910, changes were made during the campaign every year from 1911 through 1914. Apey Mills gave way to Lou Hobbs in 1911, Rudy Kling was replaced by Burt Kite in 1912, Thomas Stouch lost his job to Lonnie Noojn in 1913 and Louis Cook was fired in favor of Jack Corbett in 1914. As it turned out, Corbett was a survivor. The skipper also played second base and was idolized by Thomas Wolfe. In fact Nebraska Crane, a fictional baseball player who became a Major Leaguer in Wolfe's *The Web and the Rock* and *You Can't Go Home Again*, was based on Corbett, making the skipper the only player Wolfe wrote about directly in his numerous novels. Corbett was known as a steady fielder with a suspect bat and a keen mind for managing. Wolfe described the skipper as "strong, simple, full of earth and sun."

A half-century later, at the age of eighty, Corbett recalled Wolfe during an interview with Bob Terrell of the *Asheville Citizen-Times*. "He was my bat boy until we got in the park," Corbett said. "Then he would shag a few flies during batting practice, and disappear into the stands to watch the game."

Corbett managed the Tourists for the final home game of the 1916 slate when Asheville and Winston-Salem played what is believed to be the fastest game in professional baseball history. With Charlotte having already won the second-half crown in the North Carolina State League, the game had no playoff implications. The Twins arrived at Oates Park at noon for the scheduled two o'clock start when the visitors' manager, Charles Chaney, approached Corbett about his team's desire to catch a train that left Asheville shortly after three.

"I didn't want Charley and his boys to have to lay over so I agreed to getting the game over with as quickly as possible," Corbett told Terrell. "We really made a farce of it, but it was a regulation game of nine full innings and counted in the standings."

The teams began play at 1:28 p.m., thirty-two minutes ahead of schedule. The umpire, Red Rowe, arrived at Oates Park about twenty minutes prior to the slated game time, only to find the contest in the fourth inning. The final out was recorded at 1:59, with the Twins declared the winner by a final score of 2–1. The game time of thirty-one minutes was some sixty seconds faster than the recorded shortest contest in professional baseball annals, a Southern Association matchup in which Mobile defeated Atlanta, 2–1, on September 19, 1910.

A History of Professional Baseball in *Asheville*

According the *Asheville Citizen* a day later on August 31, 1916, "Nobody let a ball get by. Everyone hit the first ball pitched, or lobbed over, which is correct. Nobody was left on the bases. If a man hit and didn't come home, he contrived to get tagged out by overrunning the bag."

The most unusual play of the game took place in the top half of the third inning. Asheville pitcher Doc Lowe delivered the ball before his catcher was behind the plate. The Winston-Salem batter singled to center field and tried to advance to second base when the outfielder's throw headed toward the visitors' dugout. Frank Nesser, the Twins' on-deck hitter, snagged the ball and threw out his teammate with a perfect peg to the keystone sack.

Asheville team president L.L. Jenkins was none too happy when he arrived at the ballpark just in time to see the two teams conclude the day's activities. He offered to refund the ticket price to any of the estimated two hundred fans in attendance and gave both Corbett and Chaney an earful regarding his opinion of their scheme. With many of the fans realizing what had taken place, refunds were limited to a small handful.

Corbett moved on to manage Columbia in 1917, the same year World War I interfered with the baseball slate. Asheville nearly lost baseball after

The Asheville Royal Giants were the city's first black baseball team, formed by Edward W. Pearson Sr. The Royal Giants played at Pearson's Park and Oates Park. *Pack Memorial Public Library, Asheville, North Carolina, North Carolina Collection.*

the team operated more than $7,000 in the red during the previous season. The only saving grace was the successful sale of several players to teams at higher classifications and a special sale of reduced priced tickets late in the campaign. With Fred Kent providing the ballpark free of charge for the 1917 season and S.A. Lynch overseeing the team's operations, the Tourists under Doc Ferris won twelve of their first twenty-eight games before disbanding along with the Raleigh Capitals on May 18, twelve days before the rest of the North Carolina State League ceased operations.

The city was without affiliated professional baseball until 1924, although a few attempts were made to keep the baseball flame burning. Asheville, Oteen and Kenilworth formed teams and played organized amateur games in 1919. Two years later, the Western North Carolina League was revived from 1909 and resumed the previous hard feelings. Late in the 1921 campaign, Canton folded due to financial problems. Hendersonville, meanwhile, claimed Asheville and Brevard joined forces to set up a

An advertisement in the *Asheville Citizen* on May 16, 1929, promotes a game between the Asheville Black Tourist and the visiting Cuban Red Sox at McCormick Field. Even with segregation in full force in the late 1920s, the crowds included many white fans for the black baseball contests. *Asheville Citizen-Times.*

post-season championship series. Upon hearing Hendersonville's claims, Canton found some additional players and returned to the race. An "unauthorized meeting" of team representatives declared Canton the victor over Hendersonville by virtue of a forfeit, which gave Asheville, known as the Skylanders during the 1921 and 1922 slates, the second-half crown and the berth to meet Brevard in the playoffs.

Asheville and Brevard had played five games by the time the Hendersonville team took the matter to the courts. A judge ruled that neither Asheville nor Hendersonville was the second-half champion since the regular season had not been played to a conclusion. Strangely enough, the Western North Carolina League overcame such discord to survive another season in 1922 and actually flourished. Hendersonville, winners of the first half, gained some revenge by outlasting Asheville, the circuit's second-half champs, in a playoff series deemed worthy to all parties. That series would prove to be Hendersonville's last hurrah in the professional ranks until a two-year stint in the Western Carolina League in 1948 and 1949 before disappearing completely from the minor league scene.

Perhaps the most consistent performers during the late 1910s were the Asheville Royal Giants, the city's first black baseball team. Formed by Edward W. Pearson Sr., the Royal Giants played at Pearson's Park during the middle part of the decade before moving to Oates Park during the latter half and the early 1920s. The Royal Giants were a strong and stable club that faced teams throughout the South and formed significant rivalries with Atlanta and Greenville.

History has not been kind to the Royal Giants and the Asheville Black Tourist and other Negro teams during the first half of the twentieth century. Little is known about the clubs due in part to the lack of newspaper accounts. Sports editors of the day complained that the teams never called in their scores, yet one wonders how often the white press made any attempt to provide coverage of the games. Still, the teams attracted significant crowds in the black community, including contests played at McCormick Field after the facility opened in 1924. One of the more notable series took place on May 17–18, 1929, when the Asheville Black Tourists hosted the Cuban Red Sox for three games. The Cubans were one of the premier minority teams, playing fast-paced games with a variety of baseball antics that included "shadow ball" exhibitions.

Second Inning

*T*he 1920s roared throughout the United States, and few cities partied louder than Asheville. With its extravagant resorts, the area welcomed many of the rich and famous to town, and the city was determined to keep pace, particularly throughout downtown. Asheville became second only to Miami among southeastern cities in the construction of Art Deco architecture. The decade produced such famous structures that survive to this day as City Hall, the Jackson Building, First Baptist Church and the S&W Building. Surrounding farmland also became neighborhood developments, including Grovemont, Kenilworth, Malvern Hills and Beverly Hills.

Baseball also benefited from this boom. To date, Asheville's entries into professional baseball had been as secure as a cookie jar at a day-care center while toiling in ballparks that were thrown up like circus tents with field terrains that were better suited for a Civil War battle than baseball. Still, the game persevered, and the city's leaders possessed the type of political vision rarely seen since in the Land of the Sky.

With cramped Oates Park deemed unacceptable for professional baseball, the General Assembly passed a bill in May of 1923 authorizing the city commissioners to acquire property and build an athletic field. After giving strong consideration to five sites, the commissioners decided that fifteen acres of Buchanan property, owned by Wilbur Devendorf and Frank Barber and valued at $30,000, would be the most prudent place. The location for the athletic field, which became the first municipality-owned park in the city, was selected because it resided a few blocks from Asheville High School and the business district. The primary use of the land was slated for the high school football team. No longer would the school have to pay to use it, as was the case at Oates Park.

A month after the site was selected, on June 16, 1923, Frank L. Conder, Asheville's Commissioner of Public Works, proposed that the new athletic field be named for Dr. Lewis M. McCormick "as a permanent memorial" to the former city bacteriologist. The Board of City Commissioners voted to accept Conder's recommendation, approximately ten months before the ballpark opened its gates for the initial contest.

Lewis McCormick, known as "The Fly Man," never saw a baseball game at the storied site that continues to bear his name. A well-traveled researcher, McCormick worked for the city for nearly sixteen years prior to his death on January 8, 1922, at the age of fifty-eight. He received numerous offers for jobs in perhaps more exotic locations during his tenure in Western North Carolina, but the doctor always said he "loved Asheville too well to leave."

Born in 1863 on a Virginia farm just south of Washington, D.C., McCormick attended Oberlin College in Ohio. He worked with the Smithsonian Institute upon graduating from college, and during his tenure there he teamed with three other of the country's most renowned specialists in original research work in the deviation of the species. McCormick later was employed with the New York Zoological Association and began traveling the world.

Along the way McCormick faced some remarkable near-death experiences. He was in the Philippines when war was declared by the United States and narrowly escaped the charging enemy patrol by outrunning the competition for two miles before leaping into a motorboat he had hidden in the bushes. Another close call came in the South Sea Islands, where McCormick was surrounded by cannibals. He disguised himself as a native by staining his body with the juice of berries and other vegetables in order to slip past the angry mobs.

McCormick, who moved to Asheville in 1904, ventured deep into the jungles of Africa and the northern reaches of India in his search of plant and insect specimens. His studies and acumen led to his becoming known as the world's highest authority on the biology of flies. In the city laboratory, he made an exact reproduction of a fly's foot, some five hundred times the natural size.

His claim to fame in Asheville occurred when McCormick became the first man in the United States to make a scientific fight against the housefly. He approached the Buncombe County Medical Society with his proposal in 1905 and requested $1,600 to help rid the city of its burgeoning problem with the fly. The doctor proposed to use the money to improve the cleanliness of the city's large livery stables located throughout the downtown area, where, McCormick wrote, "I believe that 99 percent of the house flies that annoy the citizens breed."

When word of McCormick's "Swat That Fly" proposal spread, the doctor became the target of some ridicule. Yet, with the help of the *Asheville Citizen* and City Council, McCormick convinced the public of the disease and danger carried by the pests. He directed that the city's stables be cleaned regularly and sprinkled liberally with kerosene. The same regulations held true for privately owned barns within the city limits as well as stagnant ponds and garbage dumps. Kids armed with fly swatters visited houses and businesses to kill thousands of flies.

The fly population dwindled noticeably throughout the summer and into the autumn. Over the next five years, Asheville's annual typhoid fever rate fell from eighty-nine cases to two. National and international attention followed, with Asheville garnering a reputation as a healthful place to visit or live, thereby providing a significant boost to the city's tourism industry.

McCormick was a beloved city employee who was described as a man of high ideals, modesty and reserve. He also was instrumental in protecting the city's water and milk supply, with his establishment of Asheville's first rigid milk inspection credited with saving the lives of countless infants in Buncombe County.

Lewis McCormick was the only city bacteriologist in Asheville history. McCormick Field was named in his honor following his death in 1922. *Pack Memorial Public Library, Asheville, North Carolina, North Carolina Collection.*

Initial reports indicated McCormick died at Biltmore Hospital as a result of eating poisoned fruit. It was later determined that his death was the result of heart disease. Flags flew at half-mast and the city fire bell somberly tolled fifty-eight times, once for each year of his life, as McCormick was buried in Asheville's Riverside Cemetery on a snow-clad hill on Wednesday, January 11, 1922. Fittingly, McCormick shares the same resting grounds of fellow noted Ashevillians Thomas Wolfe and O. Henry.

Had he lived to see the ballpark, McCormick in all likelihood would have approved. McCormick Field was capable of hosting baseball and football games, with intercollegiate gridiron contests slated for the upcoming fall. A cinder track for races, barnyard golf and a shooting range for both pistols and rifles made the facility the primary home for athletics in Asheville. *Southern Tourist* wrote in its June 1924 edition:

> *This is the best and most complete athletic field in the South, and the only one this side of Washington that has an electrically equipped score board. This score board is far superior to the one in Washington.*
>
> *There are fully equipped dressing rooms and shower baths for both teams, and private rooms for the officials. There is a ladies' rest room with maid and attendant. The plumbing used at this field is the most sanitary, being of the class used in the best hotels of the country.*

The building of the new ballpark led to Asheville's acquisition of another baseball team for the 1924 season. In 1923, a financial bloodbath led to Columbia forfeiting its South Atlantic Association franchise, which played its home games in Gastonia, North Carolina, after July 26. Gastonia wanted to keep the team, only to have Dan W. Hill present a $2,500 check to the league directors in a December meeting to move the team to Asheville. Hill returned to the mountains as the team's sole owner before offering the club to the Asheville Chamber of Commerce.

With Hill named president, the team operated under the chamber's watchful eye for the next five years. The club, known as the Skylanders and Skyers before Tourists was formally approved in June 1925, entered into a loose working agreement with the Detroit Tigers, which led to the Major League club christening McCormick Field on April 3, 1924. The Tourists also received some pitching help from the Tigers, most notably Sam Gibson and George Smith, who were sent to Asheville from Detroit by manager Ty Cobb.

A crowd of 3,199 attended the first official game at McCormick Field. (There were other contests played in the new facility prior to the Tigers' arrival, with the Skylanders hosting Weaver College on March 27 and

Bingham Military Academy on April 1.) The ballpark glistened, and a large set of temporary stands were placed in center field to handle the expected overflow crowd. Yet while partly cloudy skies roofed the warm Asheville afternoon, the grandstands between first and third bases were full, but the covered seating in left and center field was sparsely occupied.

The Detroit Tigers arrived in Asheville aboard a special train at 11:00 a.m. on Friday, April 3. After lunching with the Rotary Club, the club went straight to McCormick Field to prepare for the afternoon's tilt. It did not take long for the new ballpark to receive its reputation as a hitter's haven. The short dimensions, a low rail fence that enclosed the outfield and the relatively high altitude contributed to the fly ball frenzy. In addition to the 32 runs scored in Asheville's shocking 18–14 triumph over the Tigers, home runs rained upon the banks throughout the game's duration.

Tigers left fielder Heinie Manush clubbed the first round-tripper in the ballpark's history, his first of two on the day. Detroit right fielder Harry Heilmann amazed those in attendance by peppering the roof atop the left-field stands with a pair of big flies before clearing the structure with a third monstrous blow. Cobb manned the middle garden and added another round-tripper. All three flycatchers would later be inducted into the National Baseball Hall of Fame. Larry Woodall also showed some muscle, even though he hit only one home run in ten Major League seasons with Detroit. Asheville first baseman Lefty McCrone went deep on two occasions during the contest.

The Skylanders also met the Toledo Mud Hens and the Buffalo Bisons in the spring of 1924. The team was slated to play the Atlanta Crackers before "scheduling difficulties" prevented the game from taking place. Most observers felt it was more than a coincidence that the Crackers' announcement came shortly after the Atlanta club learned of Asheville's victory over the Tigers.

Their early success notwithstanding, the Skylanders finished fifth with a 58–63 record in the six-team Class B South Atlantic League in 1924, even with Lefty McCrone leading the league with 28 home runs and pitcher Sam Gibson whiffing a circuit-best 140 batters. The Tourists were again also-rans in 1925, placing fifth in the eight-team loop with a 66–63 mark. Yet nothing created greater anticipation in Asheville in 1925 than when the New York Yankees and Brooklyn Dodgers headed for the mountains in April.

By the mid-1920s, Babe Ruth was one of the country's most popular celebrities. The Major Leagues' first prolific home run hitter, Ruth was the most dominant player of any sport at any time in the United States, and his efforts were a major reason why the New York Yankees emerged as the most dominant team of any era. Ruth's imminent arrival in Asheville created quite a stir for a city accustomed to high-profile visitors.

The Yankees were working their way north from spring training in Florida during the first week of April of 1925. The tradition in those days had teams playing exhibition games for approximately two weeks while riding the trains to the Northeast to open the regular season. The Yankees and Dodgers were slated to meet in a series of contests, including stops in Atlanta, followed by Chattanooga on April 5, Knoxville on April 6 and Asheville on April 7, prior to Opening Day on April 14. The games produced excitement at every stop. Little did anyone know in the days leading up to Ruth's arrival that Asheville would serve as the dateline for one of the country's most notable stories of the mid-1920s.

Ruth had not been feeling well since he celebrated his thirtieth birthday on February 6, 1925. His weight had increased significantly over the past few years, topped off by an eating and drinking binge since the end of the 1924 campaign that left Ruth tipping the Toledoes at a robust 255 pounds. In an effort to drop some weight, Ruth reported to Hot Springs, Arkansas, in February for a combination of exercise and steam baths. His

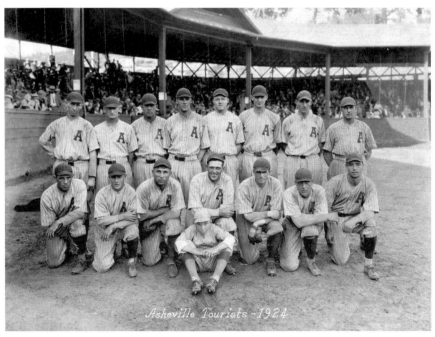

The 1924 Asheville Skylanders defeated the Detroit Tigers, 18–14, in the first official game at McCormick Field. The Skylanders went on to post a 58–63 record that season. *Pack Memorial Public Library, Asheville, North Carolina, North Carolina Collection.*

girth-reducing efforts proved fruitless before he headed for spring training in St. Petersburg, Florida.

The Babe often caught the flu before spring training, yet in 1925 his annual illness did not hit him until he reached Florida. He battled his health for most of March until the team ventured north at the end of the month. On the way to Atlanta, Ruth complained of chills and fever. He continued to fight through his conditions in Chattanooga, where he thrilled the locals with two home runs after feeling too sick to take batting practice. Ruth added another round-tripper in Knoxville, only to suffer stomach cramps with a high fever shortly after the contest.

The bumpy ride along the winding tracks through the Great Smoky Mountains did little to improve Ruth's condition. The Bambino was not alone, for several of his Yankee teammates reportedly felt nauseated prior to pulling into the Asheville train station on Depot Street about noon. Ruth staggered off the train with teammates Steve O'Neill and John Levi in front of a large crowd that had gathered to meet him. The Babe fainted, and had O'Neill and Levi failed to catch the falling star, Ruth would have been seriously injured had his head landed on the station's marble floor.

The Asheville team became known as the Tourists midway through the 1925 season. The Tourists placed fifth that year with a 66–63 record. *Pack Memorial Public Library, Asheville, North Carolina, North Carolina Collection.*

A History of Professional Baseball in *Asheville*

The Yankees made plans to ship Ruth to New York along with scout Paul Krichell. In the meantime, an unconscious Ruth was carried to a taxi and driven to the Battery Park Hotel, where outside fans and members of the media held a vigil in hopes that the Great Bambino would overcome his ills.

The show went on in Asheville without Ruth, and the Yankees had little difficulty taking care of Brooklyn, winning 16–8, with a reported eight thousand fans shoehorned into McCormick Field. New York's Bob Meusel hit a pair of home runs and scored four times as part of his four-for-four performance at the plate. First baseman Wally Pipp started for the Yankees, yet would later that season give way to Lou Gehrig, who proceeded to play in 2,130 consecutive games.

While the Yankees and Dodgers departed Asheville on the train shortly after the conclusion of their game, Ruth remained at the hotel overnight in the care of Dr. A.S. "Charles" Jordan, who determined the ballplayer was suffering from a severe intestinal attack and symptoms of flu. Jordan said Ruth needed complete rest, but the Bambino ignored the doctor's orders and departed on a train the following afternoon. With little information to report, rumors started to circulate, including one in London that stated Ruth had died. Another report had Ruth suffering a double skull fracture upon collapsing in a bathroom and hitting the basin. Anyway, Ruth reached New York at 1:30 the following afternoon. The Boston Braves feared the worst upon their arrival to Grand Central Station when they saw Ruth through a train window being removed on a stretcher.

Sportswriter W.O. McGeehan of the *New York Tribune* described Ruth's ailments as "the bellyache heard 'round the world." Ruth's bellyache, however, proved to be much more than a virus or a temporary case of indigestion. Shortly after his arrival at New York's St. Vincent's Hospital, the Babe underwent surgery for what was described as an "intestinal abscess." He spent seven weeks in the hospital, from April 9 through May 25. Amazingly, Ruth took the field shortly thereafter, playing in his first game of the 1925 season on June 1.

Legend says that Ruth's primary ailment was acute indigestion, caused by consuming too many hot dogs, soda pop and beer on the train ride between Knoxville and Asheville. Rumors also circulated that the slugger owed gamblers approximately $7,700. Those close to the situation, including Yankees general manager Ed Barrow, said privately that his primary problem centered on a bad case of venereal disease.

Regardless of what bothered Ruth, he overcame the problem. In 1925 he hit .290 with 25 home runs in 98 games, numbers that represent one of the lower outputs of his laudable career. A year later, in 1926, Ruth and the Yankees again returned to Asheville, only to leave the locals disappointed a second time. The Yankees were slated to face Brooklyn for a pair of exhibition games, but a constant downpour washed away any chance of playing ball, forcing the two Major League teams to continue their northern-bound route without taking the field. Ruth, meanwhile, rebounded during the 1927 season to hit a career high of 60 home runs while posting 164 RBIs. His legend continued to grow by leading the Major Leagues in homers every year through the 1931 campaign, which also marked a third visit to Asheville by the Babe and his buddies.

Third Inning

In the latter half of 1926, the Asheville Chamber of Commerce and the Asheville Real Estate Board produced a forty-four-page guide entitled *Live and Invest in the Land of the Sky*. The book showcased the recent completion of the Flatiron Building, the ongoing construction of the Grove Arcade with a projected price tag of $1 million and the development of Montford Hills, "the Suburb in the City" where sixty houses had been built and remaining lots were as low as $1,250. On page six, "Asheville's City-Owned Baseball Park," McCormick Field, was pictured above a description of the locals, which read: "Asheville is made up of thoroughly human, likeable folks. There's a simple, unrestrained charm about them which reaches out to the heart of the newcomer who can readily find friends of his own kind."

This statement, in so many words, would be repeated countless times over the next eight decades by those newcomers who earned their pay for play at the ballpark.

The Asheville Tourists finished in second place in the South Atlantic Association in 1926 and tied for fourth in 1927. In between the two campaigns, in December of 1926, the National Association of Professional Baseball Leagues held its annual winter meetings at the Battery Park Hotel in Asheville. Then, in 1928, under the leadership of manager Ray Kennedy, the Tourists established the franchise record by winning 97 games against only 49 losses, 18 games better than the second-place Macon Peaches. Eight Tourists, headed by Kennedy, the loop's Manager of the Year, were named to the circuit's year-end all-star team. Others included shortstop Ben Chapman, outfielders Allen "Dusty" Cooke and Stan Keyes, catcher Roy Luebbe, utility man J.W. Watson and pitchers Bill Harris and Harry Smythe.

Off the field, Dan W. Hill, who served as president of the Piedmont League throughout the first half of the 1930s, and fellow team board member E.C. Greene understood how to win friends and influence people in professional baseball. In the late 1920s, as Pack Memorial Public Library and a new courthouse were completed in Asheville, a stream of baseball dignitaries came through town. Lured to the area to mix business with pleasure were baseball commissioner Kenesaw Mountain Landis, National League president John Hydler, American League president E.S. Barnard, International League president Conway Toole and New York Yankees business manager E.G. Barrow.

Despite the tireless efforts of Hill and Greene as well as other officers and directors of the chamber of commerce, paying the baseball bills often proved difficult. Ironically, the toughest campaign on the ledger sheet proved to be the team's best showing on the diamond. In what proved to be the chamber's last season as owner, the 1928 Tourists sold six key players at the end of the slate in order to satisfy their financial troubles. Rarely did such an act take place with a Class B league, and Kenesaw Mountain Landis traveled to Western North Carolina to investigate matters. Landis gave the sales his blessing when he realized how talented the team had been.

Among those shipped out were Ben Chapman and Dusty Cooke, both of whom were sold to the New York Yankees. Chapman batted a lofty .336 with 105 runs scored, 183 hits, 32 doubles, 17 triples, 7 home runs and 98 RBIs. Cooke was equally effective, hitting .362 with 112 runs, 188 hits, 30 doubles, a league-record 30 triples, 13 circuit clouts and 96 RBIs. Others sold included Joe Heving and Joe Marty to the Yankees, Bill Harris to the Pirates and sixteen-game-winner Harry Smythe to the Phillies.

Chapman played fifteen years in the Major Leagues and batted at a .302 clip during his career. He also managed the Philadelphia Phillies from 1945 to 1948 before being replaced on an interim basis by Cooke, who played eight seasons in the big leagues. Despite being older than most of his teammates while in Asheville, the twenty-seven-year-old Heving pitched thirteen seasons at the game's top level.

Other contributors included right fielder Stan Keyes, who thrilled Asheville fans for three years, from 1927 to 1929, and averaged .340 at the plate, 94 runs scored, 165 hits, 18 home runs and 99 RBIs during that stretch. He debuted in Asheville by hitting .320 with 22 home runs and 94 RBIs before setting the table for the league champion Tourists in 1928 by

Dusty Cooke was one
of several players sold
by the Tourists to Major
League clubs after the
1928 season. Cooke
hit a South Atlantic
Association–record 30
triples prior to being
sold to the New York
Yankees. *National
Baseball Hall of Fame
Library, Cooperstown,
New York.*

hitting .330 with 15 round-trippers and 95 RBIs with 108 runs scored. He
then led the league with a .377 batting average in 1929 while earning his
second all-star recognition in as many seasons.

The Tourists fielded numerous stars during the latter half of the 1920s,
but the stretch from 1925 to 1929 is known best as the "Struttin' Bud"
Shaney era in Asheville. A World War I veteran and a pitcher with a
showman's flair, Shaney was on the verge of reaching the Major Leagues
after a strong showing at Milwaukee in the American Association when
he came down with malaria and lost more than thirty-five pounds in the
spring of 1925. He was sent to Asheville and spent the next five seasons
with the Tourists.

The durable right-hander could have outlasted Methuselah, averaging
256 innings a year in his time with Asheville while winning 85 of 146
decisions, including 23 victories in the 1928 championship season. It was
not unusual for him to toss both games of a doubleheader or be accused of
throwing a less-than-kosher cowhide, and he always attracted strong crowds

with his outstanding ability and over-the-top personality. His control was pinpoint, which was no small feat for a hurler whose primary offerings were a shine ball he learned from Eddie Cicotte of the Chicago White Sox and a spitball he garnered from Jeff Tesreau of the New York Giants. "With my speed and strength, those were all the pitches I needed besides the curve, and I could always throw the curve," Shaney said.

Often referred to as the "Strutter," Shaney gained his nickname after breaking his leg while playing football in high school. The leg was not set properly, causing Shaney to walk with a hitch that resembled a strut. His strong personality, which was perfect during the frequent moments when opponents complained about the legality of his pitches, fit his nickname like tongue-and-groove paneling. Wrote Bob Terrell in the *Asheville Citizen* in 1970, "He was of the old school, a man who spat on the ball and threw the juicer, who rubbed the ball on his wool trousers until he slicked one side and threw the shiner. He was accused of doctoring the ball with every imaginable device, because his pitches were so effective, but he denies that."

After leaving Asheville, Shaney twirled for St. Augustine, Florida, and spent two seasons with the Charlotte Hornets before returning to town in 1934 and going 3–3 in twelve games. He was back in the Land of the Sky in 1941 and lost his lone appearance. Shaney then pitched for Hickory in 1942 before returning to Asheville after his twenty-two-year baseball career came to a close. He was a bail bondsman, an athletic director, a professional umpire and the McCormick Field groundskeeper at various times. He pitched one game a year in 1953, 1954 and 1955 for the Tourists, the last one taking place at the age of fifty-five.

As South Atlantic Association champions in 1928, the Tourists featured speed and power, posting a .304 batting average with 240 doubles, 112 triples and 109 stolen bases. With no outfield fence to keep hard hits from entering the bushes on the McCormick Field bank, batters circled the bases while desperate fielders searched fruitlessly for the ball among the brush. Asheville manager Ray Kennedy led the league with a .366 batting average, topping second-place Dusty Cooke's norm. Bud Shaney went 23–11, and Joe Heving led the league with a 2.46 ERA on his way to a 14–7 record. Bill Harris provided assistance by going 25–9 with a 3.36 ERA, and his .735 winning percentage led the SAA. Harris had gone 12–7 in 1926 with the Tourists and only 3–5 with Asheville in 1927.

Struggling to operate the team despite its on-field success, the chamber decided to sell the club to a group headed by Hall F. Corpening in May 1929 for $22,000. A resident of Asheville for seven years at the time of the purchase, Corpening operated several bus lines that served the city, a fact that figured to save the team money since travel was its greatest expense.

A History of Professional Baseball in *Asheville*

Even though the Tourists were the reigning South Atlantic Association champs, the new ownership pledged greater commitment to scouting and signing younger and more talented players, which was a facet of the operation the chamber was unable to fulfill due to constraints on time and knowledge. The team also received a ten-year lease to McCormick Field, granting the Tourists use of the facility on every game date, beginning at noon, for an annual cost of $1,000. Corpening had lights installed in 1930 and the team played a handful of contests under the arcs even though day games remained the norm.

The chamber of commerce believed the new arrangement guaranteed Asheville fans professional baseball of "Class B caliber or higher" for the next decade. The scenario failed to materialize, however, due to the onset of the Great Depression. The city was hurt most when the Central Bank and Trust Company, the major holder of county funds, battened down the hatches on November 20, 1930. Buncombe County all but collapsed, with its holdings plummeting from nearly $180 million in 1927 to $80 million in

Johnny Allen led the South Atlantic Association with 173 strikeouts and earned league all-star honors as a member of the Tourists in 1929. *National Baseball Hall of Fame Library, Cooperstown, New York.*

1933. The city and county accrued a massive debt, with Asheville retaining the highest per capita debt of any city in the country. The city fathers were determined to repay every penny and did, achieving the feat finally in 1977, yet at the price of urban renewal in the 1950s and 1960s.

The Tourists survived better than most minor league clubs but were unable to withstand the realities of the Depression. In 1929 Stan Keyes led the league with a .377 batting average and pitcher Johnny Allen went 20–11 with a 3.32 ERA and led the South Atlantic Association with 173 strikeouts. The right-hander won seventeen games for the Yankees in 1932 and a career best twenty for the Indians in 1936. The team shifted to the Piedmont League prior to the 1930 season when the South Atlantic Association folded its tent. Hal Sullivan paced the loop with a .374 batting average. Brevard native Cliff "Lefty" Melton, a tall, lanky left-hander known as "Mountain Music," went 5–5 in twenty-two games for the 1931 team and later won twenty games for the New York Giants in 1937.

The Tourists and the High Point Pointers disbanded on July 7, 1932. The city was without professional baseball in 1933 before regaining the sport midway through the 1934 campaign on June 7, when Asheville replaced Columbia (then known as the Sandlappers) for the second time in a dozen years.

Fourth Inning

*A*ffiliations with Major League teams were nowhere near as steadfast in the 1920s and early 1930s compared to today. After serving as a pseudo-farm club of the Detroit Tigers during the mid-1920s, the Tourists entered into a working agreement with the Pacific Coast League's Hollywood Stars in 1931 and the Louisville Colonels of the American Association in 1932. The friendships Dan Hill and E.C. Greene had with New York Yankees business manager E.G. Barrow had the Yankees considering Asheville for their spring training venue and led to the 1931 exhibition games at McCormick Field.

Five years after rain wiped out two games in 1926, the Yankees returned to Asheville in 1931. Babe Ruth and Lou Gehrig visited the Veterans Administration Hospital in Oteen on April 6, one day after the train arrived in town. The two future Hall of Famers spent a couple of hours talking with veterans of World War I. Upon taking the diamond at McCormick Field for the first time, Ruth breathed in the sweet aroma of the honeysuckle and said, "My, my, what a beautiful place to play. Delightful. Damned delightful place!"

The McCormick Field dimensions and the Tourists' pitching proved to be of little challenge to the prodigious power provided by the Colossal of Clout. Ruth began April 7 by depositing a half-dozen long fly balls high upon the embankment beyond the center field wall during batting practice. Once the game started, Ruth contributed a first-inning double that led to a run on Lou Gehrig's two-bagger before driving in a pair of tallies with a single in the second and retiring from the contest during the late innings of the Yankees' 5–2 victory over Asheville.

The New York lineup also featured future Hall of Famers third baseman Tony "Push-em-up" Lazzeri and center fielder Earle Combs. A pair of former Tourists toiled for the Yankees, second baseman Ben Chapman, who had three hits in four at-bats on his former stomping grounds, and left fielder Dusty Cooke. The other Yankees for the one-hour-and-thirty-five-minute contest included shortstop Lynn Lary, right fielder Sammy Byrd and pitchers Lou McEvoy and Big Jim Weaver, at six foot six the tallest player in baseball at the time.

For the Tourists, the most significant performance in the first game came from third baseman Lealon Breakfield, who made several stellar defensive plays at the hot corner. In the fifth inning, Breakfield scooped a roller by Lynn, tagged out Combs trying to advance to third, and then threw Lynn out at first base. Breakfield also posted two of Asheville's five hits.

The Yankees proceeded to defeat the Tourists in the next two matchups as well, upending the hosts by counts of 11–3 and 17–4 on April 8 and April 9, respectively. Ruth and Gehrig did most of the damage in the second contest by recording a home run apiece. Wrote Dix Sarsfield in the *Asheville Citizen*, "Ruth's smash was lofted to the crest of the right field embankment, while Gehrig's blow carried well, eventually landing 30 feet up the bank behind deep centerfield." Ruth and Gehrig finished the game with two hits apiece, while Dusty Cooke and Ben Chapman, members of the 1928 Asheville club, had three hits each. Henry Johnson and Lefty Gomez twirled for the Yankees, while the Tourists sent Monroe Mitchell, Lefty Melton and Mind Ormand to the mound.

In the third and final contest, Ruth hit another round-tripper, this one completely clearing the embankment above the right field wall. Gehrig recorded a double, triple and single as part of the Yankees' nineteen-hit attack, with Sarsfield writing, "Gehrig doubled to the left centerfield bank in the first, knocking in two runs, and in the third Ruth walked and scored on Gehrig's triple to far-away centerfield." Cooke had a double, triple and two singles and another ex-Ashevillian, pitcher Johnny Allen of the 1929 Tourists, pitched in relief for the Yankees and forced in a run with four walks.

Not surprisingly, Ruth was well received upon making his long-anticipated appearance in Asheville. Sarsfield wrote, "The 2,000 fans in attendance forgot baseball during the home seventh when a gang of kids mobbed Ruth and put him to work autographing baseballs, scorecards, and whatever else they carried in pants pockets, and the $80,000-a-year Babe was just one of them and entered into the full show with the enthusiasm of his besiegers."

Their work concluded, Ruth and the Yankees departed Asheville at 4:10 a.m. on April 10 and headed for Charlotte, where the New York team defeated the Hornets and pitcher Bud Shaney, 16–13. Ruth concluded his career with 714 long balls, a total that set the standard until Henry Aaron surpassed it in 1974. That's not too shabby, especially for a man that reportedly came close to meeting his maker in Asheville midway through the most remarkable career in baseball history.

The Yankees signed a working agreement with Asheville for 1933, but the Depression ended that relationship before it ever started. The only professional baseball played in Asheville that year came on April 6, when Bill Terry's New York Giants defeated the Detroit Tigers, 4–3, in front of two thousand fans at McCormick Field. The Giants scored two runs in the bottom of the ninth with the help of an error by Detroit shortstop Billy Rogell. Four future Hall of Famers played in the game: player-manager Bill Terry and right fielder Mel Ott for New York and Detroit second baseman Charlie Gehringer and first baseman Hank Greenberg.

The Columbia Sandlappers were a Boston Red Sox affiliate in 1934 when the franchise moved to Asheville midway through the season. With professional baseball back in town, the Tourists opted to become part of the game's first minor league empire, created by Branch Rickey and the St.

The only game in town in 1933 took place on April 6 when the New York Giants and Detroit Tigers met at McCormick Field. *Asheville Citizen-Times.*

Legendary executive Branch Rickey made Asheville one of his farm teams on three different occasions, during his tenures with St. Louis, Brooklyn and Pittsburgh. *National Baseball Hall of Fame Library, Cooperstown, New York.*

Louis Cardinals, beginning in 1935. The relationship with Rickey would last for much of the next two decades.

If not for the rapid response by city officials, Asheville would have lost baseball again in 1935. McCormick Field served as the spring training site for the Tourists and three other minor league teams in the St. Louis farm system. Players began arriving during the final week of March and started working out at the ballpark. In the late afternoon of March 28, several players were taking some swings when they noticed a smattering of smoke emerging from the press box. The situation was inspected with the observers determining that someone had been smoking cigarettes while watching batting practice.

That evening, a fire broke out at McCormick Field. Bolstered by some high northwesterly winds, flames destroyed the boiler room, the main

The Tourists' 1938 score card featured forty-seven ads on its two-fold, six-panel design. One ad stated: "OH BOY! Let's Go to The 'Y' for a Shower and Swim After the Game!" *Author's collection.*

grandstand and the "Negro bleachers" down the third-base line. The ticket office, refreshment stand and about half of the seven-hundred-seat "white bleachers" went unscathed. The Cardinals lost fifty uniforms and some equipment, none of which the team had insured.

Hundreds gathered at the ballpark to see what locals described as "the biggest blaze in years." A day after the fire, the cause of which was never determined, city manager George L. Hackney cleared the insurance technicalities in order to have the wooden grandstands rebuilt immediately upon receiving the lumber. Official spring training workouts for the four minor league teams started on time, just four days following the fire, while construction workers began their efforts to restore the ballpark.

The grandstands were completed over the course of the first half of the 1935 season, although most of the 3,752 fans in the home opener against Richmond resided on the grass down the foul lines and in temporary bleachers. Billy Southworth, who managed the St. Louis Cardinals in

Hall of Fame pitcher Dizzy Dean started for the St. Louis Cardinals in an exhibition game at McCormick Field on April 13, 1937. *National Baseball Hall of Fame Library, Cooperstown, New York.*

1929 and later returned to the big leagues as skipper of the Redbirds and the Boston Red Sox, took over the reins in Asheville. With Herbie Moore leading the league with an .808 winning percentage while posting a 21–5 record, the Tourists won the Piedmont League's first-half crown in 1935 before losing to Richmond in the playoffs. Southworth returned in 1936 and saw the Tourists suffer their lone hundred-loss season in franchise history.

The Tourists served as a St. Louis farm club through the 1942 season and put together the most successful five-year run in team history. Hal Anderson handled the managerial duties from 1937 through 1939, winning pennants in his first and third campaigns. Al Sherer won twenty games for Asheville during the first slate, while Sam Maggert drove in 125 runs with the help of 40 doubles. Bob Rice served as the Tourists' general manager during that time before receiving promotions that eventually landed him as the St. Louis Cardinals general manager. Rice later resided in Asheville after retiring from the game. Team president Eddie Dyer made several stellar

A History of Professional Baseball in *Asheville*

After winning seventeen games for the Tourists in 1938, Hank Gornicki returned to Asheville midway through the 1939 slate and won his first nine decisions. *National Baseball Hall of Fame Library, Cooperstown, New York.*

Catcher Walker Cooper, *right*, pictured here with his brother, Mort, hit .336 with 8 home runs and 80 RBIs for the Tourists in 1939. *National Baseball Hall of Fame Library, Cooperstown, New York.*

deals, including the sale of Sam Narron to Rochester, and later managed the Cardinals from mid-1945 through the 1950 campaign.

On April 13, 1937, the St. Louis Cardinals, known throughout the nation as "The Gas House Gang," played the Tourists at McCormick Field and defeated the hosts, 12–4, before an overflow crowd of 5,900. Dizzy Dean allowed one hit during his four-inning stint. This Tourists team proved formidable by winning the Piedmont League with an 89–50 record before falling in the fifth and final game of the playoffs to Portsmouth. Harl Maggert led the Piedmont League with a .342 batting average, 191 hits and 139 RBIs, and a year later followed in his father's footsteps by playing in the big leagues.

Hank Gornicki pitched in just 40 innings with Asheville in 1937, but his greatest contributions came during the next two seasons. He served as the Asheville ace in 1938, going 17–13 and leading the league with a 2.57 ERA. He also established the league record by tossing 308 innings and allowed only 265 hits. In 1939 Herschel Lyons owned a 12–1 mark with a league-best 1.82 ERA when he received a promotion to Rochester in the International League. To replace Lyons, the Cardinals sent Gornicki back to Asheville. Gornicki picked up where he left off by winning his first nine decisions in thirteen starts. His efforts helped Asheville win the league by twelve games over Durham before outlasting Rocky Mount, four games to two, in the Piedmont League championship series.

Gornicki excelled while throwing to Walker Cooper, one of the toughest catchers in baseball history, who received 1,223 games behind the plate at the Major League level. A hulking mountain of a man at six foot three and 210 pounds, Cooper hit .336 with 8 homers and 80 RBIs for Asheville in 1939. His claim to fame came in three World Series, when he hit .300 in 60 at-bats and led the Cardinals to the championship in 1942 and 1944.

Manager Hal Anderson was recognized with "H.A. Day" on August 18, 1939, the same day the Tourists split a doubleheader with the Rocky Mount Red Sox. Anderson went 241–180 in three seasons at the dugout helm and ranks fourth all-time in wins by an Asheville manager.

The 1940s ushered in a few changes at McCormick Field. While Municipal Auditorium was opening its doors for the first time, Seth Perkinson, a deputy sheriff in Buncombe County, started the Knot Hole Gang. Perkinson worked with many at-risk kids, and the Tourists allowed these young boys and girls the chance to attend a ballgame for free when they arrived with Perkinson.

Lights also returned to McCormick Field in 1940, ten years after night games debuted at the ballpark, only to see the facility go dark shortly thereafter. Westinghouse Electric Company installed the lights for $8,200.

Joining the Tourists as McCormick Field inhabitants were the Asheville Blues, a black team that played in the Negro Southern League and was owned and managed by C.L. Moore, one of the premier high school coaches in the Southeast. Jim Pendleton, an outfielder with the Blues who became a top shortstop in the Negro National League during the late 1940s, reached the Major Leagues in 1953 and played nearly eight seasons with the Braves, Pirates, Reds and Colt .45s. The Asheville High Maroons, led by running back extraordinaire Charlie "Choo Choo" Justice, also played some home football games at the ballpark during the first half of the decade.

The 1940 Tourists' home schedule was found on the inside of yellow and black matchbooks, including one sponsored by Burton's Sandwich Shop on College Street, an ad that boasted "Beer Cooled Correctly." According to the matchbook, Asheville's first home game of the season was against Charlotte on April 17, with the finale taking place versus Richmond on August 26 at McCormick Field.

Among those twirling under the ballpark's new lights was Ken Burkhart, a Knoxville native who later pitched and umpired in the Major Leagues. Burkhart posted a 20–6 record with a 2.63 ERA and 19 complete games in 33 starts for the Tourists in 1940. He tied for the league lead in wins and topped the Class B circuit with 145 strikeouts. Supporting his efforts was Emil Verban, a consistent second baseman who hit .412 in the World Series for the Cardinals in 1944. With Asheville, Verban scored 82 times with the aid of 148 hits, including 19 doubles, while driving in 64 runners. Verban helped the Tourists battle for the league crown before finishing 1½ games behind the Richmond Colts and losing in the playoffs to Rocky Mount, 4 games to 2.

Verban returned to Asheville in 1941, and while the Tourists finished seventh with a 64–76 record in the eight-team Piedmont League, the man at the keystone sack remained undeterred, scoring 82 times again while posting 149 hits, 20 doubles and 43 RBIs. Bill Shewey led the circuit with 107 runs scored, and "Struttin' Bud" Shaney pitched the final game of the 1941 season; his catcher was Tourists business manager Bobby Rice.

While the Tourists again fielded a mediocre team in 1942, going 61–77 to finish in sixth place, the rest of the Piedmont League members complained about the long trip to Asheville. Combine that with the onset of World War II and aside from games between military personnel stationed in Asheville, including those at Moore General Hospital and the Asheville Redistribution Center, the town went without baseball from 1943 through 1945. The professional game returned in 1946 when Branch Rickey came calling for a second time in his illustrious career. Rickey always referred to McCormick Field as one of his favorite ballparks in the country, and he loved to smell the honeysuckle along the banks. As a result, the Tourists became a minor league affiliate of the Brooklyn Dodgers, the team Rickey joined in 1942.

The Tourists moved to the Tri-State League in 1946 and led throughout most of the season's first half to earn the right to host the circuit's all-star game that year. The All-Stars defeated the Tourists, 6–4, in front of 3,951 fans at McCormick Field. Player-manager Bill Sayles earned all-star honors by leading the league with 105 RBIs and was tabbed the circuit's Manager of the Year. Catcher Dick Bouknight won the Tri-State League batting title with a .367 average and was named to the year-end all-star team as well, joining shortstop Veo Story. The Tourists finished in second place with an 83–57 record before losing, four games to one, to Knoxville in the playoffs.

Ervin Martin Pavliecivich arrived in Asheville in 1946 as a shortstop of modest fielding ability and a desire to pitch. Having shortened his name to Erv Palica at the suggestion of Branch Rickey, the infielder committed eight errors in eighteen chances on May 8, 1946, but drove in the winning run to give Asheville an 8–7 victory over Anderson. The writing was on the wall for Palica, at least as far as his everyday status was concerned. Shortly after witnessing one of the worst defensive showings in baseball annals, Tourists manager Bill Sayles conversed with Rickey and decided to let Palica have his way by moving to the mound. He proceeded to post fifteen victories against only six defeats for Asheville and registered an impressive 2.51 ERA. He had found his calling, and a year later he was pitching in Brooklyn for the first of nine Major League seasons.

Bill Sayles knew something about changing scenery. He pitched early in his career and even took the mound for the United States in the 1936 Berlin Olympics while he was a student at the University of Oregon. Upon his return to the game after a stint in the service, Sayles became a manager as well as an outfielder. He earned all-star honors in the Tri-State League and batted a combined .347 with 18 home runs and 203 RBIs during his two-year stint as the Asheville skipper.

Another standout on the 1946 team was a local product, outfielder Sam Patton. The Buncombe County native attended Swannanoa High School and Western Carolina University prior to playing both baseball and basketball in the army while toiling in the canal zone. Patton had the opportunity to play alongside Terry Moore, the all-star center fielder of the St. Louis Cardinals who taught the green North Carolinian some of the nuances of manning the middle garden.

That experience led to Patton signing with the Pirates as a minor league free agent upon his release from the military. After joining Birmingham, Patton was traded to the Brooklyn Dodgers, and at his request, was sent to the Tourists. He responded to the familiar surroundings by hitting .345 and

A History of Professional Baseball in *Asheville*

Erv Palica won fifteen games for the Tourists in 1946 after moving from shortstop to the mound during the early stages of the season. *National Baseball Hall of Fame Library, Cooperstown, New York.*

A former pitcher who twirled in the 1936 Olympics, Bill Sayles was an all-star outfielder as well as a manager during his two-year stint with the Tourists. *Asheville Citizen-Times.*

The Tourists began their ten-year run in the Tri-State League in 1946. *Asheville Citizen-Times*.

earning a spot on the Tri-State League all-star team. The outfielder was well received by the Asheville fans, who tabbed Patton as the Tourists' most popular player.

"Back then there weren't any outfield fences at McCormick Field," Patton said. "We had to run up that hill and rummage through the bushes to find the ball, while the player ran around the bases. I was often accused of carrying an extra ball in my back pocket."

After the 1946 season, Patton married Asheville native Margaret Kennerly and took a job as athletic director of the American Enka textile plant. He coached in the Junior Industrial League and had a young man named Joe Gibbs, who would become the head coach of the Washington Redskins. Patton returned to the Tourists in 1947 and after serving a brief suspension for holding out, the six-foot-five outfielder hit .269 with 38 RBIs in 88 contests.

The 1947 season began with a visit of the bearded beauties of the House of David playing an exhibition game against the Tourists at McCormick Field on April 12. With flowing locks and long beards, the traveling orthodox Jewish players were talented, legitimate baseball players who amazed crowds

Swannanoa native Sam Patton was named the Tourists' Most Popular Player in 1946 after he ranked fourth in the Tri-State League with a .333 batting average. *Asheville Citizen-Times*.

The 1947 Tourists finished in sixth place in the Tri-State League with a 65–74 record. *Asheville Citizen-Times*.

with "pepper ball" and entertained the masses with their routine comedy acts. In competitive activity, the campaign saw Clem Labine, a durable and free-spirited sinkerballer who emerged as a stellar reliever with the Dodgers, start eight contests for the Tourists and post a 6–0 record with six complete games and a 2.07 ERA.

One year after he broke the color barrier in the modern Major Leagues, Jackie Robinson and the defending National League champion Brooklyn Dodgers paid a two-day visit to the Land of the Sky in 1948 for the first time in more than two decades. Plans called for the Dodgers to arrive to town via a bus after flying into Greenville, South Carolina, but a low ceiling forced the plane to land in Knoxville. Brooklyn then traveled for three hours through the mountains and a driving thunderstorm in the middle of the night and did not arrive at the George Vanderbilt Hotel until 5:30 a.m.

Thursday, April 8, proved as drab as last year's leaves with a steady rain soaking McCormick Field throughout the morning before subsiding shortly after two o'clock. Reserved seats for the game had been sold out for more than a week, and the line for general admission tickets stretched hundreds deep by noon. When the precipitation finally came to a halt, more than half of the eventual crowd of 5,500 was in the stands. Determined to play the game as scheduled, Tourists business manager Paul Jones ordered fifty gallons of gasoline poured along the infield dirt to help dry the field.

Jones's efforts proved successful. After a delay of only eighteen minutes, the Dodgers fielded a stellar batting order, beginning with Robinson and continuing with left fielder Arky Vaughn, center fielder Pete Reiser, first baseman Ray Sanders, right fielder Duke Snider, shortstop Pee Wee Reese, third baseman Billy Cox, catcher Gil Hodges and starting pitcher Ralph Branca. The Tourists countered with left fielder Sammy Sporn, second baseman Spook Jacobs, center fielder Norman Koney, first baseman Dick Massuch, catcher John Schieman, third baseman Ken Aubrey, right fielder Bill Jakielek, shortstop Russ Rose and pitcher Tom Lakos.

The Dodgers won the first game of the two-day event by a 7–2 final. Branca allowed seven hits while tossing a complete game. The pitcher also was the only player to hit a home run during the contest when he clubbed a solo shot deep into the bushes in left center field in the second inning. Robinson, meanwhile, went hitless in two at-bats, yet was well received by the vast majority of fans.

The *Asheville Citizen* reported, "Jackie Robinson, the first Negro ever to play in the Major Leagues, received a resplendent ovation from the left-field bleachers. The fact that he flied out to deep left field in his first appearance made little difference to the approximately 2,000 Negro fans attending. He

Jackie Robinson and the Brooklyn Dodgers visited Asheville for exhibition games in 1948 and 1951. *National Baseball Hall of Fame Library, Cooperstown, New York.*

showed his blinding speed in his second time up but Russ Rose, Asheville's shortstop, came up with a neat bare-hand catch and nipped him before he could reach the initial sack."

Brooklyn skipper Leo "The Lip" Durocher coached third base during the third and fifth innings of the first game. The Hall of Fame manager gave the fans their money's worth when he and plate umpire "Struttin' Bud" Shaney got into a dispute over a called strike that was not as heated as they made it appear.

A day later, on April 9, future Hall of Fame catcher Roy Campanella took the field for the Dodgers while Preacher Roe climbed the hill. Roe earned the victory over Tourists hurler Dan Bennett, who surrendered four runs to Brooklyn in the first inning of what proved to be a 10–2 decision. Pee Wee Reese went three for three at the plate for the Dodgers, and Spook

Jacobs had a pair of hits off Roe. Jackie Robinson again failed to record a hit in four at-bats, but the crowd estimated to be more than four thousand strong was far from disappointed. "The Dodgers came to town and put on a million dollar show and that's all that matters," said the *Asheville Citizen*.

The 1948 season was notable for a variety of other reasons in Asheville. The polio outbreak became an epidemic during the summer, and on August 1, the Tourists' home game was postponed and three other Tri-State League contests were moved to Charlotte. Speaking of the Queen City, Hornets general manager Phil Howser was far from a fan of the Tourists. As buds feathered the branches of bushes and honeysuckle blossomed across the bank, McCormick Field remained without a fence, and opponents tended to have more difficulty in finding the stitched sphere among the shrubs than the Asheville outfielders. That trend did not go unnoticed by the rest of the league. Howser became so enraged that he suggested the Tourists "must be hiding balls on the bank." The Asheville newspaper mentioned Howser's complaints and started referring to his team as "the Sweat Bees." Howser took his case to Major League Baseball, which ruled shortly thereafter that, beginning in 1949, all professional fields must have an outfield fence.

Stocked with talent by Brooklyn's Branch Rickey and managed by Clay Bryant, the 1948 Tourists led by as many as 26 games before winning the Tri-State League regular season by 17½ games over the Anderson Rebels with a 95–51 record prior to falling to Rock Hill in the playoffs. Bryant was considered an excellent judge of talent with an uncanny feel for knowing when to change pitchers. First baseman Ray Hickernell, who was in his third season with Asheville, hit .332 with 11 triples, 22 home runs and 139 RBIs while serving as a role model for the younger players. Outfielder Joe Belcastro paced the team with a .342 batting average, and second baseman Spook Jacobs hit .328 with 111 runs scored, 47 stolen bases and 92 RBIs. Five Tourists were named to the league all-star team, and Joe Landrum, a 17-game winner who led the league with a 2.77 ERA, went the distance in 20 of his 25 starts. Tom Lakos reached the 20-win plateau, going 21–8 with 21 complete games. Outfielder Norman Koney used his legs to hit at a .335 clip, stroke 193 hits (good for second in Asheville annals) and set the all-time Tri-State League record by scoring 145 runs.

The Tourists reached the playoffs again in 1949, finishing third with a 76–71 record before falling to Spartanburg in four games in post-season play. Outfielder Alexander Driskill earned Tri-State League all-star honors and led the league with 172 hits. Ed Head, who threw a no-hitter for Brooklyn on April 23, 1946, managed the Tourists. Clay Bryant returned to Asheville as skipper in 1950 after a one-year hiatus and led the Tourists to their fourth playoff appearance in five years. With William Samson leading

Tom Lakos won twenty-
one games for the Tourists
in 1948 and started against
the Brooklyn Dodgers at
McCormick Field. *Asheville
Citizen-Times.*

the league with a 1.93 ERA and Omer Ehlers and William Kearns earning year-end all-star honors, Asheville placed second with an 83–62 record, swept Spartanburg in three games in the first round of the playoffs and lost a seven-game series to the Rock Hill Chiefs in the championship round.

Ray Hathaway made his managerial debut with the Tourists in 1951 and continued the team's streak of strong showings. An 85–55 record was good for second place behind Charlotte, winners of one hundred games, during the regular season. Asheville had four year-end all-stars, including third baseman Claude Siple, shortstop Chris Kitsos, outfielder Bill Kerr and pitcher Jim Cater. Kitsos led the league with 134 runs, and Ralph Butler paced the circuit with a 2.68 ERA. The Tourists then outlasted Rock Hill, three games to two, in the first round of the playoffs, only to be swept by the Spartanburg Peaches in the finals.

Making the 1951 season even more memorable was another appearance by the Brooklyn Dodgers, who returned to McCormick Field for the second time in four seasons on Monday, April 9, 1951. In front of 6,579 fans packed closer than beds in a charity ward, Brooklyn sent Rex Barney and Carl Erskine to the mound, yet the visitors narrowly defeated the Tourists, 9–8, on an infield single by Roy Campanella that plated a pair of runs.

The 1951 Tourists won eighty-five games before defeating Rock Hill in the first round of the playoffs and losing to Spartanburg in the finals. *Asheville Citizen-Times.*

Campanella also clubbed two home runs, first baseman Gil Hodges went deep, and Jackie Robinson showcased his speed by hitting an inside-the-park home run, even though a three-foot-high chain-link fence had been installed in the outfield two years earlier. Don Thompson, who later sold real estate after moving to Asheville, had a hit in five at-bats.

The Tourists had a disappointing showing in 1952 by finishing with a 65–75 record that included a change of managers during the campaign, from William Hart to George Tesnow. Those difficulties led to the return of Ray Hathaway, who was back after a one-year stint at Newport News. Hathaway was named the Tri-State League co-Manager of the Year for the second time in as many seasons with Asheville after the Tourists finished second with an 83–67 record before losing to Anderson in four games during the playoffs. Fred Kipp led the league with a 2.23 ERA and earned a spot on the year-end all-star team. Catcher Joe Pignatano also was an all-star and had one of the most productive days in franchise history. On May 27, 1953, Pignatano drove in 10 runs with 3 homers, including a grand slam, in a 22–15 triumph over Rock Hill.

A History of Professional Baseball in *Asheville*

The Tourists won the Tri-State League in 1954 with an 86–54 record, 13 games better than Knoxville. Shortstop Jackie Spears, who hit .283 with 70 RBIs for Asheville in 1953, returned to town and batted a team high .329 with 24 triples and 82 RBIs. He also led the Tri-State League with 120 runs scored and 188 hits. Cuban Oscar Sierra batted .290 and drove in 104 runs. He added 36 doubles, many of which were the ground-rule variety after bouncing over the short left-field fence at McCormick Field. Lester Fessette went 22–8 on the hill.

On September 5, 1954, the Asheville groundskeeper took the mound for the home team. The Strutter, fifty-three-year-old "Struttin' Bud" Shaney, who had last played full time in 1942 while managing Hickory in the North Carolina State League, scattered four hits over five scoreless innings and beat out an infield single in Asheville's 4–0 victory. Sealing the triumph with four frames of shutout relief was the skipper, thirty-eight-year-old Ray Hathaway. None of the efforts made the late news; WLOS-TV would not hit the airwaves for another thirteen days.

The 1955 Tri-State League fell to four members—Asheville, Greenville, Spartanburg and Knoxville. Under the managerial reins of Earl Naylor,

The Tourists had reason to celebrate after winning the Tri-State League crown in 1954 by thirteen games over second-place Knoxville. *Asheville Citizen-Times.*

shortstop Dick Tracewski had his difficulties with the leather and committed forty-seven errors, most in the league, producing a paltry .927 fielding percentage. Tracewski received the wrath of the McCormick Field faithful's frustrations, yet his perseverance led to eight seasons in the big leagues and three visits to the World Series.

In the mid-1950s, the Tourists were kept afloat with the help of Community Baseball, Inc., a nonprofit corporation under the guidance of Fleming Talman. The members sold shares of stock for one dollar to help keep the team in town. While the plan worked in Asheville, the Tri-State was not as fortunate. Minor league baseball faltered throughout the country as the decade progressed due to the advent of television and air conditioning. The Tri-State League folded after the 1955 campaign, and baseball in the Land of the Sky disappeared for the next three years.

Fifth Inning

$\mathcal{S}$now dusted the mountains as well as the ballpark in the early days of April, just prior to the opening of the 1959 baseball season. For the previous three years, McCormick Field had served as home to stock car races. Jim Lowe of North Wilkesboro leased the ballpark from the city, and a quarter-mile asphalt track with a concrete retaining wall and a new set of bleachers were incorporated within the ballpark. The races were far from popular among the residents in the surrounding neighborhood, leading most to dread the constant roar on weekend evenings. The races proved profitable for the city, though, and such drivers as Ralph Earnhardt, Lee Petty, Junior Johnson and Banjo Matthews bumped and grinded around the small oval in Grand National events.

Upon baseball's return in 1959, McCormick Field received a major facelift in time for the Tourists' home opener against Columbus on April 16. The asphalt track was removed and sod was placed over the rocky remains. New additions included grandstand seats, a press box, refurbished clubhouses and rebuilt bleachers. After a three-foot outfield wall had served as the lone deterrent for reaching the hill beyond the outfield, a paneled fence decorated with colorful advertisements now gave the venerable old facility a new look and feel. A new scoreboard was erected by Emmett Goodwin, who used the wiring of confiscated pinball machines to create an elaborate electrical scoreboard that featured as much detail as any in the minor leagues. The words "McCormick Field" stood out in large yellow letters against the green wooden fence that formed the back of the first-base bleachers.

Fifth Inning

On March 5, the *Asheville Citizen* reported the purchase of a Longness clock, a four-foot-by-four-foot timepiece that was placed atop the scoreboard. The clock was sold as the same one that had graced Ebbets Field in Brooklyn before the Dodgers bolted for Los Angeles in 1957. Shortly thereafter, the *Charlotte Observer* reported a Longness clock with the same supposed lineage had been purchased for Griffith Stadium. As it turned out, some shady salesmen took a handful of ballparks as suckers.

Spearheading the return of professional baseball to Asheville was local businessman Fleming Talman, who reformed Community Baseball, Inc. Talman began matters by paying $12,000 of indebtedness from the previous regime and did so by raising $20,000 via the sale of $5 ticket books. Talman also wanted to change the name of the team and devised a contest to replace Tourists, which had been in place since 1925. He promised to reward the person who suggested the winning new moniker with a season ticket and named Bob Terrell and Al Geremonte of the Asheville newspapers and Zeb Lee of WSKY radio to the selection committee. Numerous names were recommended, among them Sky Sox, Highlanders and Skylanders. The trio went with Ridgerunners, and Terrell made the announcement in the *Asheville Citizen*. Talman was far from thrilled, particularly at the name's length, and decided to hold another contest, with this name to be voted upon. The Tourists ran away with more than 3,500 tallies, some three thousand more than the second-place Sky Sox.

Fleming Talman and manager Clyde McCullough, a former Cubs catcher, formed a team consisting of players who were not under contract with another professional club in 1959. The Tourists held spring training in Fort Walton Beach, Florida, and McCullough did a masterful job of molding the outcasts into a presentable group. The Phillies and Orioles provided a few players, yet the vast majority of new Ashevillians had been recently released. Byron Taylor, a Philadelphia farmhand, established the single-season franchise record by pitching 220 innings and led the league with 18 victories. First baseman Nate Dickerson stroked single after single between first and second bases and won the South Atlantic League batting title with a .362 average. By the end of the season, the Tourists surprised most observers by posting a 70–70 record.

Harry Fischer was a classic example of the type of player the Tourists fielded in 1959. After satisfying his taste of liquor and excitement on Saturday night, Fischer sweltered in the South Carolina sun and missed several fly balls over the course of the next afternoon in Charleston. McCullough released Fischer a day later, only to place a hurried call back to him after the team ran short of relievers. Fischer had pitched previously in his career and proceeded to post a shutout string that exceeded twenty innings. He also continued to contribute with the bat by hitting fifteen home runs as one of the last dual threats in Asheville annals.

The Tourists garnered a full working agreement with the Phillies in 1960 and posted a mediocre 62–77 record. Among those sent to Asheville was Ray Culp, a Texas flamethrower who at the time had received the largest reported signing bonus, $130,000, in baseball history. Culp started seven games with Asheville and went 2–3 with two complete games and a 9.00 ERA. He reached Philadelphia in 1963 and won 122 games in the Major Leagues over 11 seasons.

Fleming Talman and Community Baseball were not pleased with the Phillies. The consensus centered on believing the Philadelphia front office was not holding up its end of the bargain, failing to send the quality of players to Asheville in order to field a competitive team. As a result, a new ship with a familiar skipper sailed into Asheville in 1961. The Pirates shifted their South Atlantic League affiliation from Savannah to Asheville and brought with them a familiar face in manager Ray Hathaway, who had guided the Tourists on three previous occasions, the last coming during the division-winning 1954 campaign. Hathaway had a reputation for developing young players and maintaining a winning atmosphere, which proved to be the perfect recipe for the 1961 slate.

"Ray was a great guy to play for," said second baseman Gene Alley. "Very seldom did he say anything. He just wanted you to play hard and play the game the way it was supposed to be played. He didn't care for silly mistakes, but other than that he just let you play."

Hathaway provided leadership and did a remarkable job of keeping raw players pointed in the right direction. He told the *Asheville Times*, "[At this level] you can't be hard-nosed with the boys. When mistakes are made, you take the boy aside and talk to him. You can't kick down doors and show signs of temperament. When the players are treated fairly, the manager will be respected."

Another change involved the team's business operations. Community Baseball, Inc., named Jim Mills as the new general manager. Mills remained with the Tourists through the 1968 campaign, giving the city eight of his more than fifty years of service to minor league baseball.

"The 1961 team was a great team to start with in Asheville," Mills said. "My family and I loved Asheville right from the start. My wife helped in the office and my girls pitched in when we needed help. That's the way things were done back then."

Mills was encouraged by the preseason sale of book tickets that cost ten dollars for admission to twelve games, and had an inkling the season might be a success after a large crowd attended the team's workouts two days prior

Ray Culp was a bonus baby who signed with the Philadelphia Phillies for $130,000 and was sent to Asheville to begin his professional career. *National Baseball Hall of Fame Library, Cooperstown, New York.*

to the season opener. "We played last year in front of crowds smaller than were here last night," Mills told the *Asheville Times*. "If this is an indication of what it is going to be when we open here against Charleston next Thursday, it will be a banner year for us."

The team did its part by providing the locals with excitement, and Mills created a stir with numerous family-oriented promotions. Max Patkin, "The Clown Prince of Baseball," made his annual appearance in Asheville on June 8. Five days later was "Pony Night," during which a pony, two bicycles, six bats and six autographed baseballs were awarded to lucky youngsters between the ages of five and sixteen. The promotion brought 4,009 patrons through the gates. On August 8, Mills welcomed trick artist Jackie Price to Asheville. Price was known for chasing fly balls with a jeep, hitting and catching while standing on his head, firing balls from a bazooka, and demonstrating thirty ways how not to hit a baseball.

With Mills keeping the fans entertained, the players did their share by performing on the diamond. Willie Stargell's career blossomed like

This aerial view of McCormick Field was taken in 1959. The stands in left field, built for race fans, are visible. *Author's collection.*

honeysuckle in Asheville. After hitting 11 home runs in 1960 while toiling in Grand Forks, North Dakota, the slugging center fielder created a rallying cry among the Tourists' faithful, who bellowed, "On the hill, Will!" He answered those demands by depositing 22 pitches over walls throughout the South Atlantic League. Stargell also batted .289 and drove in 89 runs.

"He had 'big league' written all over him from the day he reported in 1961," said Ray Hathaway. "He was the team leader on and off the field. I can't think of any of my players who had more potential than Stargell."

Not only did Stargell lose balls on the hill, he also took aim at a particular object beyond the wall. "His favorite target was a light pole on the right-center field bank," Hathaway recalled. "He hit so many home runs to that spot that I always told him to lighten up or else he would knock that pole down."

Stargell lived near McCormick Field during his days in Asheville. H.C. and Erline McQueen owned the Ritz Restaurant and rented several rooms upstairs above the eatery. Stargell and the McQueens became close, with Erline feeding the young player steak, a variety of chicken dishes and his favorite, beef stew with rice. With the proper nurturing both on and off the field, Stargell reached Pittsburgh the season after he played in Asheville, marking the beginning of a twenty-one-year Major League

Gene Alley played second base in Asheville for the first time in his career prior to becoming an all-star shortstop with the Pittsburgh Pirates. *Bob Terrell collection.*

career that concluded with his first-ballot election to the Baseball Hall of Fame in 1988. While Stargell was the first former Tourist to achieve such acclaim, a dozen other members of the 1961 club climbed to the game's top level.

Gene Alley spent the entire 1961 season as well as part of the 1962 campaign in Asheville. A second baseman on the Tourists' championship club, he saw most of his activity at third base a year later before moving to shortstop in Pittsburgh. Alley had little difficulty handling shortstop with the Pirates because he had played that position throughout his high school days. In fact, second base was as foreign to Alley as the North Carolina mountains when he arrived in Asheville from spring training with the rest of his teammates on April 14, 1961.

"That was a hard learning experience in Asheville," Alley said. "But I was willing to play anywhere in the infield if that's what it took to reach the big leagues."

Alley has said that his primary memory of Asheville centered on taking hundreds of ground balls at the keystone sack prior to games at McCormick Field. The practice enabled Alley to emerge as one of the top defensive infielders in the South Atlantic League. He also contributed at the plate with several game-winning hits on his way to batting .263 with 14 home runs and 61 RBIs.

"We had so many good players that year in Asheville and it was a fun team to play on," Alley said. "We had a good mix of young players as well as some guys who had been at higher levels of the minor leagues and had come down."

While Alley and Stargell had the most productive Major League careers among the 1961 Tourists, many observers predicted similar success for Jesus McFarlane. The Cuban-born catcher was considered a five-tool prospect and lived up to that reputation throughout his days in Asheville. A frequent showman on the field, McFarlane backed up his swagger with production, batting .301 with 21 home runs, 92 runs scored, 74 RBIs and 27 stolen bases in 1961. He wound up spending parts of five seasons in the Major Leagues, debuting in 1962 and continuing into 1968.

"He had more ability than just about any player I ever played with," said Charlie Leonard. "I saw him have some great years and I saw times when he wouldn't put forth any effort at all. Jesus had a great arm and could run and steal bases. He had power to all fields. He was a tremendous catcher."

Another power hitter was Rex Johnston, who spent most of the 1961 season manning left field for the Tourists. Johnston already had a taste of the big time, though not on the diamond. The two-hundred-pounder from California played the previous football season with the Pittsburgh Steelers before turning his focus toward baseball. He proved equally adept in his second sport by hitting .289 with 18 home runs and 66 RBIs as a member of the Tourists and saw action in fourteen Major League games with the Pirates in 1964.

"Rex was another great athlete," Charlie Leonard said. "I was watching him play on television one day when he was with the Steelers and he tackled Jim Brown so hard that it knocked both of them out. But that's the type of player Rex was. He would run through a brick wall to make a play."

The Tourists also fielded a handful of players who contributed significantly in Asheville but failed to reach the big leagues. Headlining the list of such performers was Gary Rushing, who was drafted the previous winter by Pittsburgh out of the Milwaukee Braves' organization. Rushing spent the first half of the 1961 slate at first base while providing much of the team's power throughout the campaign. He entered the season having lost 20 pounds from the previous slate, dropping to 216. The added quickness improved his bat speed, enabling the California native to drive the ball with more consistency.

"Gary had a tremendous year," Gene Alley said. "He came out of nowhere and tore that league up. He was a big boy who could hit the ball a long, long way. He was probably the best hitter on our team that year and definitely gave our team some of its muscle."

Teaming with Gene Alley up the middle was pint-sized shortstop Reggie Hamilton. Hamilton's game was based on speed at the top of the Tourists' batting order, enabling him to hit .280 with 44 RBIs in 97 contests. He also made countless spectacular defensive plays to help solidify an outstanding Asheville infield.

"At one time, Reggie was the top prospect in the Pittsburgh organization," Alley said. "He was very athletic, a good fielder and a good ballplayer. The Pirates felt sure that he would be the next shortstop at Pittsburgh."

One of the more popular players among both his teammates and the Asheville fans was third baseman Duncan Campbell. After hitting at a .272 pace with 7 homers and 58 RBIs at Savannah in 1960, Campbell took his game to a higher level with the Tourists. By the time he was promoted to Triple-A in early August, Campbell owned a .293 batting average in 106 outings.

"He's the best third base prospect in the league and the organization," Ray Hathaway told the *Asheville Citizen* nine games into the 1961 season. "He's going to be in the big leagues—and soon." Added Rex Bowen, Pittsburgh's director of scouting, "If nothing happens, he'll be in the majors sure as God made green apples."

Unfortunately, neither Hathaway nor Bowen was correct. Something did happen. A few years after he played in Asheville, Campbell was killed in an automobile accident in Nicaragua.

The Tourists also were blessed with a deep pitching staff that changed like a chameleon over the course of the season. Tommie Sisk, who opened the slate as an eighteen-year-old starter after receiving a $40,000 signing bonus the previous summer, was one of the lone hurlers to remain with Asheville throughout the season and finished with a 12–3 mark and a 3.82 ERA.

The most notable additions were a pitcher who made the climb to Pittsburgh at the end of the season and another who never saw the lights of the big leagues. Larry Foss arrived in Asheville in late June and went 10–3 over the last two months before getting called up to the Pirates. A month prior to Foss's arrival, Jim Hardison joined the rotation and proceeded to win virtually every time he stepped on the mound. He concluded the campaign with a 16–2 record.

A History of Professional Baseball in *Asheville*

"Jim had been around for a while and really knew how to pitch," Charlie Leonard said. "He wore those hitters in the South Atlantic League out. He had an overpowering curveball and didn't throw real hard. The hitters couldn't hit him."

After starting the season by winning two of three games in Knoxville, the Tourists played their home opener on April 20 against the Charleston White Sox. According to the *Asheville Times*, Miss Margaret Ensley sang the national anthem, the Reverend W.B.A. Culp of Abernathy Methodist Church said the invocation, a Marine Corps color guard presented the colors and George Chumbley, president of the Asheville Chamber of Commerce, threw out the first pitch.

In front of a crowd of 3,453 fans at McCormick Field, the Tourists struck with ten runs in the second inning, highlighted by Gary Rushing's grand slam, on their way to a 14–8 triumph. Bob Priddy went the distance despite surrendering 13 hits and 9 walks to record his second win of the season.

Prior to the game, during a luncheon for the club and the board of directors of Community Baseball, Inc., Ray Hathaway tipped his hand for the first time. "Come September, you will be prouder of this club than any that has ever represented you here in Asheville," said the skipper. Even Hathaway could not have known how accurate those words would be.

The Tourists continued to discover success during the first homestand. Gary Rushing, who broke up a no-hitter with a home run in the ninth inning during the team's first loss of the season in Knoxville, continued to wield the hot hand with a game-winning single in the bottom of the eleventh inning to defeat Charleston, 5–4, on April 23. A night later, the first baseman added two more home runs, including the game-winning RBIs in the bottom of the eighth, to lead Asheville to a 9–8 triumph over the visiting Jacksonville Jets. Rushing then crushed his fifth long ball of the season in a 6–3 win over the Jets on April 26. By the time the team left town for its second road trip, the Tourists owned a five-game winning streak and an 8–2 record, leaving them atop the South Atlantic League standings.

After splitting a few decisions, Asheville returned to first place on May 4 by defeating Columbia, 12–10, at McCormick Field. Jesus McFarland put on another power display and tied a league record by hitting three home runs in the contest. He started the barrage with a drive that landed high on the left-field bank, an estimated 450 feet from home plate. A shot to center field followed in the third before the catcher cleared the left-field wall with a line drive in the fifth. He concluded the evening with 7 RBIs.

The Tourists improved to 12–6 on the season when Rex Johnston produced a three-run triple in the sixth inning to give Asheville a 6–5 win over the visiting Reds on May 5. After Asheville split two games with Greenville, Gary Rushing added more heroics to his resume with a game-winning homer in the bottom of the eleventh inning in a 3–2 triumph over the Spinners on May 8. The first baseman drove in all three of the Tourists' runs in the game to increase his league-leading totals to 7 homers and 28 RBIs. At that point, the twenty-three-year-old Rushing had delivered the winning hit in five of his team's first thirteen triumphs.

"I'm sure [Rushing's] not a flash in the pan," Ray Hathaway told the *Asheville Times* twenty-two games into the campaign. "He just grew up. Every player has to grow up some time, be it today, tomorrow or otherwise. That's what we wait for. He's been the man all year for us. If you had to put your finger on one individual to date, it would be Rushing. Effort? He gives you 102 percent all of the time."

Asheville remained in first place after Curt Raydon threw a complete game five-hitter in a 7–3 win at Jacksonville on May 15. Two weeks later, on May 29, Asheville received pitchers Jim Hardison and Red Swanson from Macon in the Southern Association. Two hours after his arrival, Swanson debuted with the Tourists by hurling a complete game victory at Charlotte, allowing one earned run and four hits over nine frames in a 5–1 triumph. That win enabled Asheville to conclude a short road trip with a perfect 5–0 mark, pulling the Tourists to within a half-game of first-place Greenville in the league standings.

Hardison took note of the Tourists' productive lineup and was immediately impressed. Said the right-hander, "I may not lose a game here." As with many other statements made that season, Hardison's words proved prophetic.

Asheville put together a seven-game winning streak in mid-June and became a focal point of the baseball world when Bob Bailey reported to the team after signing with the Pirates for $175,000, which was the largest reported bonus ever given to an amateur player at that time. Tommie Sisk played a role in the signing by returning to his native California to help convince Bailey, his former high school teammate, to sign. Sisk then proceeded to join Pittsburgh in Washington for an exhibition game and earned the victory in a 5–2 win over the Senators on June 19.

Sisk was back in Asheville in time to join nearly 2,500 fans as well as reporters from *Time*, *Newsweek* and United Press International at McCormick Field to see Bailey's debut on June 22. According to the *Asheville Times*, the crowd "applauded loudly" throughout the evening for Bailey, who walked in his first professional at-bat before grounding out the next three times.

Yet it quickly became evident Bailey would experience difficulty at shortstop. By the end of the campaign, he had committed 27 errors in

75 games. His problems with the leather carried over to his performance at the plate, where Bailey hit just .220 with 9 home runs and 31 RBIs. A few of his teammates questioned the Pirates' rationale in signing Bailey, especially since the move relegated the smooth-fielding Reggie Hamilton to the bench.

Charlie Leonard was among those wondering what the Pirates saw in Bailey before the two roomed together in 1962 while with Triple-A Columbus. That's where Bailey became a full-time third baseman and lived up to the lofty expectations. Pittsburgh was so impressed that the team rushed Bailey to the big leagues in only his second season. And while he remained in the Majors for seventeen years, Bailey's desire to hit a home run every time he swung the bat at Forbes Field and his lack of minor league seasoning kept him from reaching even greater heights.

"He really struggled in Asheville," Leonard said. "He'd throw the ball away about every other time and he didn't hit much. I considered myself to be a pretty good defensive first baseman but he couldn't get many throws close to me. We all wondered what was wrong. The next year I roomed with him in Triple-A and he hit .300 with 30 homers and 100 RBIs. He told me that he was in over his head and nervous while he was in Asheville. But that next year he got his bearings and produced like a bonus player would."

Of his time in Asheville, Bailey said, "McCormick Field was a place for chaos every night." While Bailey struggled, Asheville continued to receive stellar pitching from its starters. The Tourists swept a double-header from Greenville, thanks to eight strong innings from starter Don Doepker. A reliever during the season's first two months, Doepker won his first start with a 4–1 triumph at Columbus on June 16. He then won his eighth game during the lidlifter against the Spinners, mixing his fastball with an excellent dropball and curveball to help Asheville move four games ahead of Greenville in the standings.

Doepker, however, was lost for the season soon thereafter with a calcium deposit in his elbow. That ailment could have harmed the Tourists' fate if not for the efforts of general manager Jim Mills. Having noticed that reliever Ed Strichek had been released by Greenville, Mills signed the pitcher to an Asheville contract. Strichek went on to pitch brilliantly in thirty relief outings with the Tourists, tossing 74⅔ innings and allowing only sixteen earned runs for a 1.93 ERA.

The offense also came through in clutch situations. On June 24, Willie Stargell blasted a game-winning home run in the bottom of the eleventh inning to lead Asheville to a 3–2 victory over Greenville. Stargell caught fire at midseason and served as a catalyst while the Tourists won 10 of 11 contests in late June. During that stretch, the center fielder cracked 16 hits in 38 at-bats, lifting his batting average from .267 to .292. He also drove in 9 runs to increase his season total to 44 RBIs.

More help arrived on June 25 when the Tourists received first baseman Charlie Leonard from Triple-A Columbus and pitcher Larry Foss from Class A Macon. Leonard got caught in a numbers game with a Columbus club loaded with talent. Foss, meanwhile, arrived from the Southern Association, and both players became perfect fits to the championship puzzle.

A seven-hitter by Tommie Sisk during a 5–1 victory over Knoxville on July 5 gave Asheville the best record in the South Atlantic League, which meant the Tourists earned the right to host the circuit's all-star game at McCormick Field. On July 17, the Tourists played the best players from the loop's seven other clubs. A crowd of 6,603 packed the ballpark, making it the largest gathering at McCormick Field and the second-largest attendance for a South Atlantic League All-Star Game at that time. Tommie Sisk started for Asheville while Sam Ellis, a rookie sensation for the Columbia Reds, opened for the All-Stars. The Tourists led 5–4 before Columbia's Bobby Klaus drove in two runs with two outs in the top of the ninth to lead the All-Stars to a 6–5 win.

During the festivities, Jack Hairston, sports editor of the *Jacksonville Journal*, released his annual poll of South Atlantic League managers. Not unlike the present-day efforts of *Baseball America*, Hairston asked the skippers to rate the league's best prospects. Not surprisingly, Asheville was well represented. Three Tourists were deemed the best players at their position, including third baseman Duncan Campbell, first baseman Gary Rushing and catcher Jesus McFarlane. Second baseman Gene Alley, pitcher Jim Hardison and outfielder Rex Johnston placed second at their respective spots. McFarlane also was tabbed the best prospect among non-pitchers, while Rushing was selected as the loop's top power hitter. Willie Stargell was rated the outfielder with the best arm. Among the pitching categories, Hardison was considered to have the best curveball, and Larry Foss was one of six hurlers deemed to possess the loop's best fastball.

The all-star game defeat proved to be one of the few setbacks Asheville suffered during the season's last two months. Larry Foss won his second game to extend the Tourists' lead to eight with a 10–2 victory at Knoxville on July 23. Jim Hardison improved his record to 11–1 with a 9–8 win over Charleston on July 25. Tommie Sisk recorded his twelfth triumph and sixth straight win with a 6–3 decision at Charleston on July 26. Foss then picked up his third victory with a 6–5 win at Charleston on July 27, even though he was pitching one day earlier than scheduled.

Manager Ray Hathaway looks over General Manager Jim Mills's shoulder at the tickets for the 1962 season. The men are pictured with the South Atlantic League championship trophy from 1961. *Bob Terrell collection.*

"I really came on in late July and August, but our team was playing so well, we expected to win every game during the last few weeks of the season," Foss said. "There was one start I had to make a day early when the guy who was scheduled to start got sick. It was in Charleston, and the temperature was about 102 and the humidity was about the same. I lost about 13 pounds during that start, but I won the game. That's what was so nice about pitching in Asheville. It never got terribly hot there like it did in other cities around the league."

The victories continued to mount for the Tourists even after the team lost Duncan Campbell on August 6. The twenty-two-year-old third baseman, who ranked second in the South Atlantic League with 76 RBIs and fourth with 16 home runs, was called up to the injury-plagued Columbus club. Despite receiving the promotion, Campbell experienced mixed feelings, telling the *Asheville Times*, "I really hate to leave the club and all the people who have been so good to me in this town."

The *Asheville Times* reported that the feelings were mutual, stating, "When Campbell leaves the field tonight for the airport, it won't be just another ballplayer or number leaving. It will be one of the most popular players ever to wear an Asheville uniform."

Bob Bailey replaced Campbell at third base, enabling Reggie Hamilton to return to his starting assignment at shortstop. The Tourists missed nary a beat and by August 16, the race was all but over when Jim Hardison improved his record to 15–1 with a 6–2 win over Charleston. Hardison went the distance for the fourteenth time in 17 starts, with his lone setback coming during a 9–8 loss to Portsmouth on July 12. Larry Foss remained just as hot as Hardison by winning his eighth decision in a 9–1 victory at Jacksonville on August 21 and his ninth in a 5–1 triumph over Charlotte on August 27.

A graduate of North Carolina State University, Hardison overcame a sore shoulder in late August. Ray Hathaway was clear about his feelings regarding the twenty-seven-year-old Wilmington native, telling the *Asheville Times*, "He has been the savior of this club. Jim's been the stopper for us. Whenever we would lose one or two, he would go in and get us back on the right track. Hardy goes out with one purpose. That's to beat you. He's one heckuva competitor."

The Tourists clinched the pennant on August 28 when their game was rained out at Portsmouth and second-place Knoxville lost to Charlotte, 4–1. The Tourists traveled to Charlotte for four nights after departing Portsmouth. Foss improved to 10–3 on the season by tossing a no-hitter into the seventh inning of what proved to be a four-hit complete game in a 9–2 triumph over the Hornets. The team then boarded the bus after a Sunday afternoon tilt on September 3 and was greeted two hours later by a large group of fans in Swannanoa. Organized by the Shriners, a motorcade met the Tourists' bus at 8:00 p.m. and accompanied the team to McCormick Field for a large celebration.

"That was a big surprise," said Charlie Leonard. "Winning in the minor leagues is not that eventful, but the fans in Asheville really supported us. I played nine seasons in the minors and Asheville was my favorite spot. It was cooler there, and the ballpark was so picturesque. That motorcade topped off a great year for the team."

More festivities followed during the final two games of the season. Jim Mills organized "Ray Hathaway Night" during the finale on September 5. A crowd of 2,123 attended the final game, a 2–1 win over Portsmouth, bringing the season's total attendance to 96,132. The fans and players presented Hathaway with gifts, and news was received prior to the game that the night's honoree had been named the South Atlantic League's Manager of the Year. Gary Rushing was selected as the loop's Most Valuable Player, and Duncan Campbell, Jesus McFarlane and Jim Hardison were tabbed to the circuit's year-end all-star team.

There were no South Atlantic League playoffs in 1961, although the season did not end for two players. Jesus McFarlane and Larry Foss received promotions to Pittsburgh for the final month of the Major League campaign. While McFarlane did not see any activity, Foss went 1–1 with a 5.87 ERA in three starts, including a victory over the Cardinals and St. Louis ace Bob Gibson in his debut.

The Tourists never relinquished first place after June 20. Asheville spent only twenty-two days of the 1961 season in second place and twenty-one days in third. Jim Hardison led the circuit with 16 wins, which represented the league's highest total since Macon's Frank Marino went 19–1 in 1941. Gary Rushing topped the league with 25 home runs and 99 RBIs. In fact, the Tourists led the loop with 155 round-trippers, with Willie Stargell and Jesus McFarlane placing second and third in the league with 22 and 21 home runs, respectively.

"That season was a classic example of success breeding success," Charlie Leonard said. Added Larry Foss, "I don't think anyone at the time realized there would be so many guys off that ballclub who would be in the big leagues within the next year or two. But we had fun in Asheville. Aside from getting the call to the big leagues, it was probably the most fun I had in baseball."

Sixth Inning

opping the 1961 season represented a near-impossible feat for both the Pirates and the Tourists. The 1962 team featured Dick Means, who hit 36 home runs in the South Atlantic League, 27 of which came with Asheville following a mid-season deal with Charlotte. Elmo Plaskett, one of the most popular players in Tourists history, and Duncan Campbell, back for his second tour of duty at McCormick Field, also hit 27 homers that season. Steve Blass went 1–4 prior to winning 103 games in the big leagues with the Pirates.

Plaskett also outlasted Charlotte's Tony Oliva for the batting crown, .3498 to .3497. One of the deciding calls came late in the season when Asheville official scorer Bob Terrell ruled an Oliva hit that went through the legs of third baseman Duncan Campbell as an error, much to the dismay of the Charlotte team. Terrell remained adamant through the Hornets' pleas. "I never ruled a ball hit through a fielder's legs as a hit," Terrell said. "The Hornets were irate, but I told them that if the situation had been reversed with Plaskett, I would have made the very same call."

After guiding the Tourists to a 70–70 record in 1962, Ray Hathaway managed the Tourists again in 1963, going 79–61 in the South Atlantic League, just two games behind first-place Macon. Jose Martinez, who had hit four homers for the Tourists a year earlier, blossomed into a better batter in 1963 by raising his average thirty points, to .273, while swatting 20 home runs. Ambidextrous pitcher Troy Giles earned year-end all-star recognition by leading the Double-A circuit with 159 strikeouts and equaling Lynchburg's Fred Talbot with 18 wins.

A History of Professional Baseball in *Asheville*

Having served in the recent past as a farm team for Philadelphia and as a current member of the Pittsburgh organization, Asheville welcomed several former Tourists back to McCormick Field for an exhibition game. On April 11, 1964, 5,315 fans greeted the Pirates and Phillies, with Pittsburgh winning, 16–3, even though Philadelphia used Jim Bunning and Ryan Duren among their pitchers. Jesus McFarland, who would return to play for the Tourists in 1965 after toiling for the team in 1961 and 1962, showed how comfortable he was at the Asheville ballpark by hitting a home run to deep left field. Willie Stargell, Roberto Clemente and Jerry Lynch also went deep for Pittsburgh; Richie Allen and John Hernstein cleared the fences for the Phillies.

A scuffle took place when Pittsburgh first baseman Donn Clendenon applied a hard tag to the Phillies' Tony Taylor. Umpire Ken Burkhardt tossed Clendenon out of the game, which led to the emptying of both benches. Other than some pushing, finger-pointing and mild threats, the event was little more than an act of bravado on both sides.

The Tourists finished last in 1964, and Ray Hathaway was fired as manager on July 10 with Asheville owning a 28–53 record. That proved to be Hathaway's last stint as the team's skipper, and his 518 victories continued to rank first in team history through the 2006 season. Luke Walker, who later pitched eight seasons with Pittsburgh, received little support in his first year with Asheville, going 8–14 with a 3.53 ERA in 1964 before reversing his fortunes by leading the Southern League with a 2.26 ERA and 197 strikeouts and posting a 12–7 record a year later. Dave Roberts, who pitched in thirteen Major League seasons, had modest success in 1964 before returning to town in 1966 and going 14–5 while pacing the Southern League with a 2.61 ERA.

The 1965 season included the return of Jesus McFarlane and Elmo Plaskett. McFarlane, who displayed power and speed while guiding the Tourists behind the plate in 1961, hit .292 with 22 home runs and 69 RBIs in his Asheville encore, which helped pave the way for another visit to the big leagues a year later, this time with Detroit. Plaskett, the South Atlantic League batting champion in 1962, hit .284 with 18 homers and 47 RBIs in 90 games before he returned to Asheville yet again in 1966, when he batted .243 with seven homers and 32 RBIs in 189 at-bats. The Tourists, meanwhile, missed a chance to win the Southern League title in 1965 when the Columbus Confederate Yankees failed to play two games due to weather conditions and finished .001 ahead of Asheville in the standings, even though the Tourists owned 80 triumphs compared to Columbus's 79.

In 1966, as Bob Caldwell made his debut at WLOS-TV on June 16, Dock Ellis won 10 games with a 2.76 ERA before winning 138 decisions in the

Major Leagues. Bob Robertson provided offensive assistance with several of his long home runs clearing the lightstand in left field. "Bob hit the longest ball I've ever seen," said Richard Morris, an official scorer at McCormick Field from 1959 through 1991 and former sports editor for the *Asheville Citizen*. "He hit it down the third-base line, over the trees beyond the left-field wall and up on the field at Memorial Stadium."

Robertson returned to Asheville as the team's batting coach in 1991, twenty-five years after he led the Southern League with 32 home runs and 99 RBIs. "This was one of my favorite places I ever played," said Robertson. "Whenever I was in a so-called slump while in the majors, I'd reflect back on my days in Asheville and the things I did here. It would really rejuvenate me."

Throughout much of the 1960s, professional baseball remained a community project, operated by a board of directors headed by chairman Fleming Talman, who owned an office supplies store on Patton Avenue. The team was anything but a profitable business, with the Pirates supporting Asheville with approximately $60,000 a year to serve as their Double-A affiliate. By 1968, B&B Pharmacy was a sponsor of the team in a relationship that would last more than three decades, and Three Brothers Restaurant was a new eatery that advertised with the team and boasted an air-conditioned dining room and parking for 242 cars. Tickets to Tourists games were $1.75 for reserved seats and $1.25 for general admission. Ice cream, popcorn, peanuts and Cracker Jacks were 15 cents each at the McCormick Field concession stand, while hot dogs and large soft drinks sold for three dimes apiece.

The Pirates' departure after the 1966 season led to the Tourists' one-year association with the Houston Astros in the Carolina League. Mike Daniel was one of four pitchers to lead the loop with fifteen wins. Catcher Hal King topped the circuit with 30 home runs and was joined on the league's year-end all-star team by Dan Walton, who tied for fifth on the circuit with a .302 batting average. The team, however, finished in last place in the Western Division with a 64–74 record.

After one season as an Astros affiliate, Asheville signed a three-year agreement with the Cincinnati Reds, beginning in 1968. Poor pitching led to a 6–11 start before manager George "Sparky" Anderson's moundsmen rebounded to form the best relief corps in the Southern League. Aiding the hurlers was the loop's best defense. The infield eclipsed the century mark in double plays due to the incredible range of shortstop Frank Duffy, who arrived in Asheville during the first week of May and moved Darrel Chaney to second base. Chaney also contributed at the plate by leading the Tourists with 23 home runs and 79 RBIs, despite hitting at just a .235 clip.

A History of Professional Baseball in *Asheville*

Darrel Chaney formed a superb double-play duo with shortstop Frank Duffy and provided power with 23 home runs and 79 RBIs for the Tourists in 1968. *Asheville Tourists.*

The offense also received contributions from outfielder Bernie Carbo and his 20 round-trippers and 67 RBIs. An even greater surprise came from left-handed hitter Arlie Burge. While in the army the previous fall, the outfielder learned he needed glasses. He added spectacles to his wardrobe and led the league with a .317 batting average.

"These glasses have helped," Burge told John Pardon of the *Asheville Times*. "I can see the rotation of the ball better and the ball looks bigger. That's gotta help. And I can wait longer on the pitch. I get a better look at the ball."

While Burge stroked line drives to all fields, the Tourists caught fire behind 16-game winner Grover Powell, who had pitched for the New York Mets in 1963, and reliever Dan McGinn, who had a string of 23 consecutive outings without allowing a run. Asheville won 10 of 12 games versus Birmingham and Montgomery, beginning June 29. Sparky Anderson

George "Sparky" Anderson guided the Tourists to the 1968 Southern League pennant two years before he was named manager of Cincinnati's "Big Red Machine." *Asheville Tourists.*

then guided the Tourists to 22 triumphs in their final 29 contests to win the eighth pennant in franchise history. The clincher came at Charlotte when the Tourists topped the Hornets, 7–5, behind Don Anderson's 5 hits and 5 RBIs on August 31. The champagne flowed in the visitors' clubhouse, with general manager Jim Mills in the middle of the celebration.

"This is a better club than we had in '61," Mills told reporters. "We have more prospects." While Sparky Anderson moved to the Major Leagues in 1969 as a coach with the San Diego Padres, ten players from the championship club would play at the game's top level. Mills also left Asheville after eight seasons to become general manager of the Spartanburg Phillies in 1969. In 1977 Mills was tabbed president of the

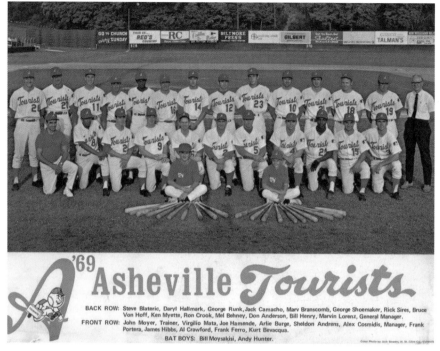

'69 Asheville *Tourists*

BACK ROW: Steve Blateric, Daryl Hallmark, George Runk, Jack Camacho, Marv Branscomb, George Shoemaker, Rick Sires, Bruce Von Hoff, Ken Myette, Ron Crook, Mel Behney, Don Anderson, Bill Henry, Marvin Lorenz, General Manager.
FRONT ROW: John Moyer, Trainer, Virgilio Mata, Joe Hamende, Arlie Burge, Sheldon Andrens, Alex Cosmidis, Manager, Frank Portera, James Hibbs, Al Crawford, Frank Ferro, Kurt Bevacqua.
BAT BOYS: Bill Moysakisi, Andy Hunter.

The 1969 Tourists went 69–69 in the Southern League under manager Alex Cosmidis. *Asheville Tourists.*

Carolina League and was later inducted into the North Carolina Sports Hall of Fame.

"I loved Asheville and that club and found more pure enjoyment in the minors than in the bigs," said Anderson, who guided Asheville to an 86–54 record. He took over the Cincinnati Reds in 1970 and managed 26 seasons in the Major Leagues, becoming the first skipper in history to win a World Series in both the American and National Leagues. Anderson retired ranking third all-time with 2,194 victories, behind only Connie Mack and John McGraw, and was elected to the Baseball Hall of Fame in 2000.

Despite the team's performance on the field, attendance at McCormick Field fell to 43,324 in 69 home dates. By comparison, twenty years earlier the Tourists attracted 122,693 fans while capturing the flag in the Tri-State League. There was little improvement in the stands in 1969, although the diamond gems continued to come through town. Don Anderson led the league with a .324 batting average and 100 RBIs, and third baseman Kurt Bevacqua ranked second with a .316 batting norm and made numerous stellar defensive showings at the hot corner.

Don Anderson led the Southern League with a .324 batting average and 100 RBIs as a member of the Reds organization in 1969. He returned to Asheville as a member of the White Sox in 1971. *Asheville Tourists.*

Dave Concepcion had 100 hits while playing in 96 games with the Tourists and paced the Southern League shortstops with a .939 fielding percentage. A year later he became the starting shortstop in Cincinnati and remained a catalyst for the Big Red Machine for nearly two decades, winning five Gold Gloves and leading the club to back-to-back World Series titles in 1975 and 1976.

"I wasn't in Asheville very long, but I was very happy there," Concepcion said. "The people treated me very good and the area was very nice. Asheville is my kind of town. I would sign autographs at a local high school whenever I could and the S&W Cafeteria was my favorite place to eat. We had a good team in one of the toughest leagues to play in. Asheville helped me prepare for my years with the Reds."

The Reds' final season in Asheville, the 1970 campaign, was unlike the first two. The Tourists finished in last place with a 59–80 record under skipper Jim Snyder, and the team attracted a trifling 28,720 patrons, also last in the Southern League. The situation improved somewhat in 1971 when Asheville became a Chicago White Sox affiliate. Larry Sherry managed the Tourists, who competed in the Southern League, which joined the

Texas League to form the Dixie Association. Ken Hottman established the Tourists' single-season home run record with a league-best 37 and also paced the loop with 99 runs and 116 RBIs. Catcher Vic Correll went deep on 22 occasions, and James MacDonnell topped the circuit's pitchers with 17 wins and 5 shutouts. Asheville won 90 games, yet finished a game and a half behind Charlotte in the standings. The Hornets then defeated the Tourists, two games to one in the playoffs.

The White Sox moved to Knoxville after their one-year stint in Asheville. With Fleming Talman heading the negotiations again, the city struck a deal to serve as the Double-A affiliate of the Baltimore Orioles. Part of the agreement with Baltimore included Asheville changing its name from Tourists to Orioles (or O's, for short), which the club leaders reluctantly agreed to. The city also had to give McCormick Field a $30,000 facelift that included construction of the right field bleachers, a new grandstand roof and improved lighting. The restrooms and clubhouses were rebuilt, with the home locker room known as the "Bird House." The seats were repainted an Oriole orange with black trim.

Another change involved the team's front office. Al Harazin, an industrious young Cincinnati lawyer, became the Asheville general manager and invested $10,000 in the team. Harazin was aggressive and determined to make baseball games at McCormick Field a better experience for the fans. His additions included hiring an organist, employing ball girls and fielding an Oriole mascot named "Ozzie."

One of Harazin's first duties as general manager involved making a call to John Dawson, who was serving as the Asheville Little League commissioner in 1972. Harazin realized the deadline for sign-ups in West Asheville for Little League Baseball had come and gone, yet pleaded with Dawson to make an exception for a couple of youngsters named Cal and Billy Ripken, who were the sons of new Asheville manager Cal Ripken Sr. Dawson had little idea the impact the twelve-year-old Cal would have on the diamond. Playing shortstop and pitcher, Ripken led his team to the state championship title. Said Earl Cobb, who coached the winning West Asheville team, "He was head and shoulders above the other boys. He just lived for playing baseball. There was no messing around when he was on the field."

The seeds of what proved to be Major League careers for both Cal and Billy were planted over a three-year span at McCormick Field. The two made a habit of hounding the likes of Doug DeCinces, Al Bumbry and Rich Dauer with questions regarding their insights in playing the game. Rusty Pulliam, a current real estate developer in Asheville, remembered working with Cal Jr. in the Orioles' dugout. "Cal would watch every game from behind the backstop to learn what pitchers were throwing," Pulliam said. "Then after the fans and players had left, he would ask his father questions about what happened in the game and why."

"Our times in Asheville were some of the most memorable days of my childhood," said Billy Ripken, who arrived in town at age seven. "We would have dinner at 2:30, before Pop would head off to the ballpark. We ate together as a family and most of the time the topic at the dinner table would be about baseball. My heroes were the players in Asheville, because that's all I knew. I'd get home from the ballpark and turn on the television and the lead story was the Asheville Orioles."

Cal Ripken Sr. executed "The Oriole Way" to an art form. His face weathered and creased as barn wood, the baseball lifer spent thirty-six seasons as a player, scout, coach and manager in the organization, including three years with the Double-A players in Asheville. In his first season with Asheville, in 1972 Ripken guided the team to the Southern League regular season pennant before losing to Montgomery in the playoffs.

One of the first impact players to hit town under the Baltimore banner was center fielder Al Bumbry. Bumbry volunteered to serve in the Vietnam

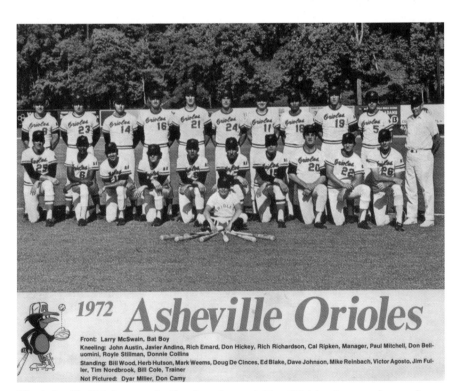

The Asheville Orioles won the Southern League's East Division in 1972, the team's first year under the Baltimore banner and manager Cal Ripken Sr. *Asheville Tourists.*

A History of Professional Baseball in *Asheville*

War prior to the start of his professional baseball career and won a Bronze Star for meritorious service. He played just 26 games in Asheville prior to being promoted to Triple-A Rochester, yet the leadoff hitter served as an early catalyst for the team that finished in first place. Considered one of the fastest players in the minors, Bumbry stole 10 bases and drove in 10 runs while posting a .347 norm in 121 at-bats. He earned Rookie of the Year honors in the American League in 1973, became the first Oriole to post 200 hits in a season, and established the Baltimore record for stolen bases.

On June 12, 1972, Mike Reinbach had one of the most prolific days in Asheville annals. Reinbach produced 6 hits in 6 trips to the plate and drove in 9 runs to lead Asheville to a 17–1 victory over Columbus. The UCLA product won the league's Most Valuable Player award as well as the Triple Crown with a .346 batting average, 30 home runs and 109 RBIs while also pacing all league hitters with 123 runs, 169 hits and 301 total bases.

In three seasons as manager of the Asheville Orioles, Cal Ripken Sr. posted 222 wins, good for fifth in franchise history. Ripken is pictured here talking with "Struttin' Bud" Shaney. *Asheville Tourists.*

His marks for runs and total bases established single-season marks in the Southern League.

Fleming Talman resigned as chairman of Community Baseball after the 1972 season. Known throughout the town as "Mr. Baseball," Talman entered the diamond fray in 1954 and was the primary reason the professional game returned to Asheville prior to the 1959 slate. Bob Terrell wrote in the *Asheville Citizen*, "For many years Talman has kept baseball in Asheville, many times with his business acumen and other times on the strength of his name, his word and his personality."

Talman gave way to George Chumbley, a vice-president of First Citizens Bank, as president of Asheville AA Baseball, Inc. The team broadcasted thirty games on WKKE 1380 AM, where the listeners heard the Orioles produce yet another batting champion in 1973 when Rob Andrews led the Southern League with a .309 average and topped the circuit with 98 runs scored and 167 hits. Terry Clapp led the league with 35 homers, at the time the second-highest total in Asheville history, and 98 RBIs.

In 1974, when twenty-four-year-old Jim Duffy replaced Al Harazin as the team's general manager, Rich Dauer hit .328 prior to playing ten years for Baltimore. The 1974 season proved to be Ripken's swan song in Asheville

Community Baseball, Inc., sold stock to local businesses and baseball fans in order to keep the Tourists financially afloat in the 1950s, 1960s and 1970s. *Ron McKee collection.*

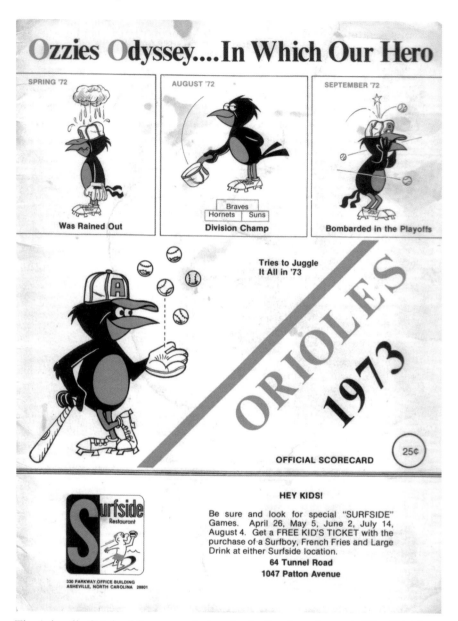

The Asheville Orioles fell to second place in the Southern League's West Division in 1973 despite the offensive dominance of Rob Andrews and Terry Clapp. *Ron McKee collection.*

as well as the minor leagues. He made the move to the Major Leagues for the remainder of his career after going 965–795 as a minor league skipper, including a 222–194 mark with the Asheville O's.

The Orioles and Asheville went through a divorce that included some finger-pointing during the final weeks of the 1975 season. The fans were unimpressed with the lack of contending teams during the last three seasons, and the Baltimore brass was far from enamored with the playing facilities. Nevertheless, there was some talent that came through town during the final season.

Mike Flanagan started eleven games with Asheville to open the 1975 season, going 6–4 with a 1.82 ERA and seven complete games. He reached Baltimore by the end of the year and won the American League Cy Young Award in 1979. Two months after Flanagan departed, Asheville fans got a glimpse of Dennis Martinez after he had gone 12–4 at Miami in the Florida State League. The Nicaraguan pitched in 6 games for the McCormick Field dwellers, going 1–4 with a 2.60 ERA. Known as "El Presidente" in his native country, by the time he retired in the late 1990s, Martinez owned more Major League victories than any other Latin-born pitcher in the game's history.

Few observers realized in 1975 how talented a player Eddie Murray would become. The first baseman arrived in Asheville late during the 1974 season for seven at-bats before returning a year later. Only nineteen while in Asheville, Murray struggled for most of the campaign while batting exclusively from the right side. Orioles manager Jim Schaffer's remedy for players experiencing hard times centered on having them hit from the opposite side of the plate during early afternoon drills. Murray revealed he had tried switch-hitting in Little League, yet was not allowed to follow such pursuits in high school or as a professional.

For three weeks Schaffer watched Murray drive the ball as a left-hander during batting practice prior to home games. Finally, late in the season, after Murray had struck out against Knoxville's Tim Stoddard, Schaffer told his pupil to give his left-handed swing a shot in game competition. Murray took two strikes before dumping the third pitch into left field for a hit. The Baltimore brass was less than pleased upon hearing the news, but the results were undeniable. Murray concluded the Southern League season earning all-star recognition upon hitting .264 with 17 home runs and 68 RBIs, and was the American League Rookie of the Year in 1977. The future Hall of Famer hit home runs from both sides of the plate in the same game in a Major League record eleven times during his career.

"It was a tough fight for Eddie and myself until everybody started believing it," Schaffer said. "I remember Cal [Ripken Sr.] said, 'You can't

A History of Professional Baseball in *Asheville*

Asheville Orioles manager Jim Schaeffer encouraged Eddie Murray to try switch-hitting in 1975. Initially, the Baltimore brass was not enthusiastic about the skipper's suggestion. *Asheville Tourists*.

Eddie Murray learned to switch-hit during the waning days of the 1975 season while in Asheville. That skill led to Murray's induction into the Baseball Hall of Fame. *Asheville Citizen-Times*.

do that; you'll get fired.' I said, 'That's OK. It's something I believe in. And even more importantly, it's something Eddie believes in, too.'"

While the Orioles took their toys to Charlotte, Fred Nichols, a thirty-two-year-old resident of Madison, Connecticut, and president of CTT Financial Services, moved his Anderson, South Carolina franchise in the Class A Western Carolinas League (in 1980, the circuit was renamed the South Atlantic League) to Asheville. Nichols renamed the team the Tourists and brought with him a working agreement with the Texas Rangers. The situation proved fortunate for Asheville baseball fans, for times were tough once again throughout the minor leagues, even as they celebrated their seventy-fifth anniversary. Some Major League clubs suggested reducing or even eliminating the costly player development setup, and with little funding many minor league teams succumbed to their financial burdens. The Western Carolinas League served as a prime example, with Asheville's arrival giving the circuit its fourth team. With only the Tourists, Greenwood Braves, Charleston Patriots and Spartanburg Phillies on the roll, the WCL was forced for the second time in as many years to play an interlocking schedule with the Carolina League in 1976.

Merrill Eckstein began his run as the team's general manager during the United States' bicentennial, including a midnight fireworks show at McCormick Field as the calendar changed from July third to the Fourth. Ten quarter-beer nights and double-headers with college teams playing several times prior to the professional tilts highlighted the slate. Under the supervision of Asheville Parks and Recreation director Ray Kisiah, McCormick Field received another new coat of paint along with a new Tourists clubhouse and additional improvements to the concession stand.

The 1976 season also brought the debut of Wayne Terwilliger as Asheville's manager. "Twig" had been in the professional ranks since 1948 and reached the Chicago Cubs a year later. Known for his hustling approach to the game, Terwilliger began managing with Greensboro in the Carolina League in 1961. His stay with the Tourists would be four seasons, during which he won 305 games, the second-highest franchise total at that time.

From an individual standpoint, the changes in affiliation and league did nothing to alter the results, for Asheville fielded two Triple Crown winners in the team's first two seasons with the Rangers. In 1976 the terrific cannonade of Pat Putnam earned the first baseman *The Sporting News* Minor League Player of the Year award as well as the distinction of becoming the first player in Western Carolinas League history to win the Triple Crown. He batted .361 with 100 runs scored, 194 hits, 33 doubles, 24 homers, 142 RBIs and 305 total bases. His marks for hits, RBIs and total bases set

A History of Professional Baseball in *Asheville*

Gene Ochsenreiter reveals the Asheville team will be renamed the Tourists for the 1976 season. Sitting beside Ochsenreiter is General Manager Merrill Eckstein. Community Baseball President George Chumbley is standing in the back. *Asheville Tourists*.

Wayne Terwilliger ranks third in Asheville history with 305 wins as the Tourists' manager. *Asheville Tourists*.

single-season records for the WCL and remained the standard for the South Atlantic League through the 2006 campaign.

When not at McCormick Field or on the road in 1976, Putnam could be found at Bee Tree Lake. He woke up early most mornings and spent the day fishing prior to reporting to the ballpark. "I didn't know exactly what the league records were at the time; I was just trying to do the best I could," Putnam said. "For some reason Texas kept me in Asheville for the entire season and I think that is why my records still stand. Usually when a player is having that kind of season, they get called up."

Putnam was far from the lone contributor on the team that won the Western Carolinas League crown by a game and a half over the Greenwood Braves in 1976. Wayne Terwilliger's group featured LaRue Washington, who led the league with 106 runs; Harold Kelley, who had a league-best 13 wins and a 3.02 ERA; and Paul Mirabella, who posted a circuit-high 136 strikeouts. Danny Darwin joined the Tourists in early June after signing as a non-drafted free agent. He went 6–3 with a 3.62 ERA for Asheville and was pitching in the Major Leagues two years later.

The Tourists were looking to break the fifty-thousand mark in season attendance during the last half of the 1970s. *Ron McKee collection.*

A History of Professional Baseball in *Asheville*

David Rivera then won the league Triple Crown in 1977 by hitting .346 with 26 home runs and 118 RBIs while leading the league with 176 hits and 25 stolen bases. Rivera also played in the Western Carolinas League All-Star Game that was held at McCormick Field and won by the South, 8–3, behind the bat of Ozzie Virgil Jr. That same season the Tourists' Greg Jemison scored 126 runs and stole 82 bases to set the franchise single-season marks. Dave Righetti established an Asheville record with 201 strikeouts while going 11–3 with a 3.14 ERA. Four years later he was the American League Rookie of the Year, and six years later, on July 4, 1983, Righetti tossed the New York Yankees' first no-hitter since Don Larsen threw a perfect game in the 1956 World Series. Their performances, however, were not enough for the Tourists to pull out the Western Carolinas League title despite going 81–58 to finish one game behind the first-place Gastonia Cardinals.

First baseman Jim Barbe nearly gave Asheville a third straight Triple Crown winner in 1978 when he led the league with 18 home runs, 99 RBIs and 143 hits, yet fell just shy in the batting race to Greenwood's Steve Hammond. Barbe spent much of the summer sending Spartanburg native Wayne Tolleson racing around the basepaths. Tolleson was an All-American wide receiver at Western Carolina University before he turned his attention on a full-time basis to baseball. He hit .269 with 21 RBIs and 19 stolen bases for the Tourists and reached the Major Leagues in 1981 with the Rangers.

Jamie Farr led the Western Carolinas League with fourteen wins in 1979, and the Tourists finished in second place with a 75–63 record, three games behind Greenwood. Merrill Eckstein had solid clubs as a Texas affiliate, yet the love was not reciprocated by the Asheville fans. Eckstein did everything he could to keep the team financially afloat, including a fundraising drive that garnered the support of thirty-one local businessmen to buy the club from Fred Nichols after the team drowned in red ink in 1977. Eckstein revived the efforts under the heading of Tourists Baseball, Inc., and sold $10,000 worth of stock for $100 a share. He paid off the team's $5,000 debt and used the remaining money to operate the club. Yet those dollars proved as fleeting as skywriting on a windy day, which forced Eckstein to look at more drastic measures.

As luck would have it, one of Eckstein's final moves with the Tourists proved to be his best.

Seventh Inning

T he world was a different place in 1980 compared to the present. The Internet, e-mail and cell phones were nothing more than space-age ideas. Ronald Reagan had recently unseated Jimmy Carter as president of the United States, *Ordinary People* won Academy Awards, and Asheville's population was tabulated at 54,022.

Professional baseball, meanwhile, bordered on being a nonentity in the Land of the Sky. The Tourists had attracted 42,012 fans in 1979, the same year Bele Chere began its run that would become the Southeast's largest free outdoor festival. The majority of what few fans showed up possessed the same feeling that made the Christians go watch their buddies wrestle with the lions while using McCormick Field as a place to drink beer and shout profanities and racial slurs at the players. The growl of dark clouds representing baseball's permanent rainout in Asheville were ambling across the sky and gaining force.

Hercules's task of cleaning out the Augean stables was mere child's play compared to the job confronting Ron McKee in 1980 when Merrill Eckstein hired the used-car salesman as general manager of the Tourists. Yet with constant assistance from his wife, Carolyn, the McKees established law and order at the aging ballpark, all the while handling nearly every chore to open the gates on game day.

"I guess what I remember most about that first year was the experience with some of the fans," McKee said. "There weren't that many people at the games. We'd have maybe 400 or 500 fans a night, and even less than that on Mondays, Tuesdays and Wednesdays, and I couldn't believe how much trouble they were. There were a few events that weren't particularly pleasant, but I was determined to make things better. I started with the attitude that I was hosting the fans at my house."

Working in baseball had been a dream of Ron's since he served as a Tourists batboy in 1961. Nevertheless, neither he nor Carolyn had any experience in operating a club. The majority of Ron's background had come on a car sales lot; Carolyn sold real estate. Yet when the opportunity at the ballpark presented itself in the waning days of 1979, the couple decided the job was worth the risk.

Ron was the Tourists' lone employee in January of 1980. He soon discovered he needed assistance, which led to Carolyn providing help any way she could. Ron called on a few friends for advertising and ticket sales before widening his scope throughout Asheville. Even though baseball was not held in the highest regard on the city's entertainment front, as natives of the area and graduates of Asheville High, Ron and Carolyn received enough early support to make progress.

"Being from here and knowing people here, we got a lot of help from a lot of people," McKee said. "I think maybe some people felt sorry for me, knowing that we had four kids and a mortgage and everything else. But we got a lot of backing from the media, especially from WWNC and from Larry Pope at the newspaper. A lot of positive things happened with the help of others, and that got some momentum rolling."

McKee admitted he did not have a clear picture of what he was getting into at the ballpark. He and Carolyn had attended only a few games at McCormick Field during the 1970s. But after garnering as much advertising revenue as he could in three months while Carolyn balanced the books, and the kids—Catherine, Chris, Ken and Matthew—organized tickets on the dining room table at home, the McKees were ready for Opening Day in April of 1980.

"I remember everything was a blur because I was so nervous," McKee said. "I don't remember whether it was hot or cold. I just remember this feeling of almost panic right before the game."

The Tourists attracted 49,066 fans in 1980, an increase of more than 7,000 from the previous year. Not only did the McKees clean up the atmosphere by eliminating the rowdies, they handled every other aspect as well. About 2:00 p.m. on game days, Ron started boiling the water to cook the hot dogs and began popping the popcorn before a concession worker or two arrived at 5:30. He also came up with the trivia question, then turned it over to Carolyn, who typed it on the insert sheet and printed it on a mimeograph. Carolyn also got the money together before heading downstairs to sell tickets from the lone window.

Ron McKee was named general manager of the Tourists during the latter part of 1979 and held the position until Larry Hawkins was promoted prior to the 2005 campaign. *Asheville Tourists*.

"Our offices upstairs were two rooms," Carolyn said. "It was too cold to work in there during the winter, so we moved everything to our house. There was a door that divided the two rooms, but we took it out in order to fit a couple of folding chairs in Ron's office for when he had visitors. I put up some curtains in there and put down some carpet on that nasty floor. It was quite a scene, but it's all we had."

While all of the McKee children would work at the ballpark, they were not allowed to leave the office during games early on. The crowds were simply too unpredictable. The kids instead used every square inch of the office floor to stretch out their sleeping bags while Ron policed the facility and Carolyn counted the receipts.

"I remember the first time we had The Chicken here," said Carolyn, referring to August 11, 1987, when a McCormick Field record 7,583 fans attended the game against Myrtle Beach. "I'd never seen so much money in my entire life. The kids enjoyed it here, and I think they did just about every job at one point or another. We wouldn't let the girls be batboys. They didn't think that was fair, but we knew it was in their best interests."

A History of Professional Baseball in *Asheville*

Even with the help of only a few game-day employees, times were tight for the Tourists. While Ron drew a salary from the club, Carolyn's payment for the 1980 season was a trip to baseball's winter meetings in Texas. In fact, the McKees departed for Dallas with less than a dollar in the checking account. Had it not been for a check that arrived as pre-payment for advertising while they were gone, Ron would not have been paid in December.

The situation improved steadily over the next few seasons, with the biggest influx coming in 1982 when Peter "Woody" Kern purchased the Tourists for $17,000 and paid off $25,000 in debts. Kern bought the stock owned by Miles Wolff, who had purchased part of the team from Merrill Eckstein and the local businessmen to become the sole owner. While many people thought he was crazy to spend such a large amount of money on a club that teetered on going out of business, Kern provided the team with some operating capital for ballpark repairs. He also kept the McKees in charge. Those efforts paid dividends over time, as evidenced by the thermometer on the side of the McCormick Field grandstand that kept a running tally of the campaign's attendance. Ron stared at the sign and wanted nothing more than to reach the top, which represented sixty thousand fans for a single season.

To the surprise of many, the McKees reached and exceeded that once-lofty goal in 1981. The Tourists welcomed 70,957 fans to McCormick Field, thanks to the improved atmosphere as well as popular promotions instilled by Ron, headlined by Thirsty Thursday. Attendance varied slightly until 1986, when the Tourists won the South Atlantic League's North Division and hosted 101,962 patrons to the ballpark.

By 2005 the McKee's sweat equity led the Tourists to become the most stable franchise in the South Atlantic League. During his last several years as general manager, McKee kept a framed picture of the team's 1980 baseball cards in his office. When he looked at the individual images, he mentioned former players and coaches as if they were family—pitcher Tony Fossas and first baseman Pete O'Brien toiled in the Major Leagues for many years; pitcher Kerry Keenan went on to serve as a college coach in Florida; catcher Donnie Scott became a coach in the Cincinnati Reds' farm system; trainer Joe Nemeth moved to Salinas, California; coach Andy Hancock died too young.

"There were a lot of good memories for us," Ron said. "It's amazing how fast time goes by. There were some ups and downs along the way, but I wouldn't trade what Carolyn and I experienced for the world."

Meanwhile, on the diamond at McCormick Field, Tom Henke joined the Tourists during the 1980 season and posted an uninspiring 0–2 record with a 7.83 ERA. He returned to town in 1981 and showed the stuff that enabled him to save 311 games at the Major League level. Employing an overpowering fastball that clocked in at 95 miles per hour and a filthy forkball that produced its fair share of strikeouts, Henke showed promise at the back end of the bullpen during his second tour of duty, going 8–6 with a 2.93 ERA in 28 outings prior to a promotion to Double-A Tulsa.

When asked of his memories regarding his days in Asheville, Henke recalled mostly the efforts of teammate Danny Murphy, who was named the South Atlantic League's co-Most Valuable Player with Greensboro's Jeff Reynolds in 1981. "I remember sitting in the bullpen and watching Murphy get hit after hit," Henke said. "We kept saying to ourselves, 'If this guy gets one more hit, he's probably going straight to the big leagues.'" While Murphy paced the circuit with a .369 average, and pitcher Darryl Smith tied for the league lead with sixteen wins, it was Henke who made the Majors within a year after his last appearance with Asheville.

After Randy Braun led the South Atlantic League with twenty-three home runs in 1982, the Tourists changed affiliations again, yet maintained their Texas ties by joining the Houston Astros' organization for the second time in Asheville annals. Tracy Dophied led the cheers by pacing the league with 27 home runs, and fan favorite Charlie Kerfeld, a hard-throwing, fun-

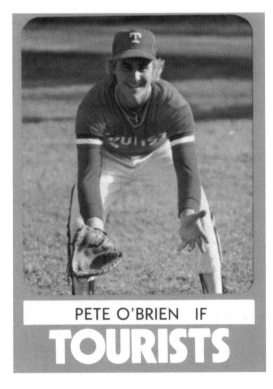

PETE O'BRIEN   IF

TOURISTS

Pete O'Brien was named the South Atlantic League's all-star first baseman in 1980. *Author's collection.*

loving right-hander, earned all-star recognition while topping the SAL with 16 victories. Two Tourists tossed 1–0 no-hitters during the 1983 season, with Arbrey Lucas accomplishing the feat versus Columbia on June 13 and Richard Strasser mirroring the effort against Anderson on July 16.

Though it would become antiquated within a decade and cursed by Tourists fans due to its inability to remain completely lit, a new scoreboard was installed prior to the 1984 campaign. Though basic in design, the scoreboard was put up in conjunction with the Miller Brewing Company and measured thirty-eight feet by twenty-eight feet and contained more than two miles of wiring and 1,123 lamps. The total cost, including installation, was $40,000.

The split-season format helps champions in the minor leagues emerge from the most unlikely places. The Tourists benefited from the setup in 1984, rebounding from a mediocre 31–41 showing during the first half to challenging for the South Atlantic League crown in August and September. The parent Houston Astros sent some reinforcements in shortstop Bob Parker, outfielder Chuck Jackson and outfielder-catcher Mark Reynolds. The pitching staff, specifically starters Anthony Kelley, Greg Dube, Rob Mallicoat and Steve Verrone and relievers Tom Funk and Ed Reilly, displayed more consistency. Despite never winning more than four straight games during the season, the Tourists moved into first place on July 22 when Kelly and Reilly combined to shut out Spartanburg, 1–0, in twelve innings. Two weeks later, on August 5, Asheville defeated Anderson, 3–1, at McCormick Field to take over the North Division lead for good before clinching the crown with a 7–3 victory over Spartanburg on August 24.

Asheville faced Greensboro, North Division winners in the first half, in a best-of-three playoff battle. With newcomer Mark Reynolds clubbing a two-run homer and Dave Dyrek driving in three runs, the Tourists won the series lidlifter at McCormick Field by an 11–9 count. The series moved to Greensboro's War Memorial Stadium, where the home team won the first game, 3–1, before the Tourists rallied from a two-run deficit to beat the Hornets, 4–3, in eleven innings. Chuck Jackson drove in the winning run in the top of the eleventh, and Rob Mallicoat and Ed Reilly handled the twirling efforts from the mound.

The Tourists advanced to the championship series against the Charleston Royals where their good fortune continued. Playing at College Park in Charleston, the hosts jumped out to a 7–0 lead after 4 innings before an extended downpour washed the results away. Asheville took advantage of the new lease on life by winning the next day, 5–4, in eleven innings, with Jackson again providing the game-winning RBI. Mallicoat and Reilly combined to give the Tourists the victory in Game Two with a 9–2 decision.

The series moved to McCormick Field for Game Three, with the Tourists rewarding more than 1,300 fans by pounding out 16 hits in a 7–2 win and a three-game sweep for the South Atlantic League title. Reynolds homered in all three games, while Greg Dube was the winning pitcher in the finale by fanning nine batters in six innings. Tom Funk sealed the victory with three innings of shutout relief.

The influx of new blood proved to be the difference down the stretch and helped guide Asheville to its first outright pennant since 1968. Mark Reynolds and Bob Parker hit .305 and .302, respectively, and Chuck Jackson drove in 32 runs in 59 games. Their efforts meshed nicely with first baseman Jim O'Dell's 19 home runs and 78 RBIs, catcher Troy Afenir's 16 round-trippers and 69 ribbies and Snyder's 11 homers and 60 RBIs. Dyrek, who served as the team's leadoff batter, hit .275 and drew 113 walks. On the mound, Anthony Kelley won 14 games and posted a 2.58 ERA, while Steve Verrone won 10 outings. Funk and Reilly had 9 and 8 saves, respectively.

The 1985 Tourists had the best overall record in the South Atlantic League's North Division but finished a half-game back in both halves to miss the playoffs. For the third time in four seasons Asheville fielded the league's home run champion, with Peter Mueller pacing the circuit with 28 big flies, and outfielder Joe Mikulik topped the team with 141 hits. Pitcher Tom Funk returned to McCormick Field for the second straight season and was named to the league's all-star team, going 9–2 with a 1.74 ERA and 12 saves.

The Tourists started wearing uniform patches in the early 1980s that promoted "Baseball in the Smokies" and "The Greatest Show on Dirt." *Ron McKee collection.*

A History of Professional Baseball in *Asheville*

In 1986 Bill Stanley's Barbeque & Bluegrass was in its heyday just north of the ballpark, with the Marc Pruett Band picking and strumming every Tuesday through Saturday evening. With the big boxes not yet entrenched in the area, Ace Appliance Company celebrated its thirtieth year in business and remained the city's premier location to purchase refrigerators, televisions and the newest craze—videocassette recorders. The 1986 Tourists did not receive a championship banner for their efforts, but the team ranks among the best since the city returned to the Class A ranks in 1976.

Winners of both halves of the South Atlantic League's Northern Division, the '86 club became only the third team in Asheville annals to reach the 90-win plateau, and posted the franchise's third-highest winning percentage at .643 after prevailing in 33 of their first 42 games. Pitcher Blaise Ilsley, with his funky delivery from the left side, posted 12 wins versus 2 losses while striking out 146 batters in 120 innings. The left-hander also tossed 9 complete games and 3 shutouts and had a league-best 1.95 ERA. He allowed only 74 hits in 120 innings while issuing only 23 walks, and was named the SAL Pitcher of the Year despite pitching only half the season on the circuit.

Richard Johnson also put together a first half for the ages. The first baseman from Sam Houston State University clubbed 24 home runs with 78 RBIs in 68 games and batted a robust .396. Despite hitting from the right side, Johnson took full advantage of the short porch at McCormick Field. The right field wall resides only 301 feet from home plate, and during Johnson's era, there was no thirty-six-foot wall as there is today. Johnson hit just five big flies in the second half after a promotion to the Florida State League and never climbed above the Double-A level, where he topped out with fifteen home runs. As a result, performances such as Johnson's have caused many observers to dismiss most power numbers that come from Asheville players.

Even with Johnson and Ilsley in Osceola during the season's second half, the Tourists continued their winning ways. Manager Ken Bolek, who also lost productive third baseman Carlo Colombino to a broken jaw on July 13, mixed and matched the pieces that enabled the Tourists to win twelve of their last thirteen outings to overtake Sumter for the division crown and top the standings by seven games. The playoffs, however, proved to be a disappointment, with Asheville losing three of four games to the Columbia Mets for the South Atlantic League championship.

The playoffs notwithstanding, the 1986 Tourists gave the 102,000 fans at McCormick Field some performances they would not soon forget. Outfielder Cameron Drew was tabbed the league's Most Valuable Player and most outstanding Major League prospect after he led the circuit with 26

Joe Mikulik was a catalyst of the 1985 Tourists, some fifteen years before he was named manager of the Asheville club. *Asheville Tourists*.

home runs, 117 RBIs and a .581 slugging percentage. Houston's first-round pick in 1985 out of the University of New Haven, Drew lost the Triple Crown to teammate Carlo Colombino's .339 norm. Drew also led the league with 255 total bases and tied for the top spot with 13 game-winning RBIs. Center fielder Scott Markley batted .315 atop the lineup and stole 41 bases while leading the loop with 147 hits and 113 runs.

On the mound, Todd Credeur helped the Tourists overcome the loss of Ilsley by posting a 13–2 record with 147 strikeouts in 130⅓ innings. Terry Wells and Pedro DeLeon won 12 and 11 games, respectively, and right-hander Stan Fascher saved 12 games in a team-high 45 outings from the bullpen.

The winning ways at McCormick Field continued in 1987. The Tourists went 91–48 and finished 25 games ahead of the second-place Charleston Wheelers in the North Division before falling in five games to Myrtle Beach in the playoffs. With runners breaking from their bases like hares in a brush fire, the Keith Bodie–managed club stole a league record 335 bases and became known as the "Bodie Bandits." Shortstop Lou Frazier had 75 thefts despite missing 30 games with a dislocated finger. Outfielder Bert Hunter swiped 56 bags, left fielder Tuffy Rhodes accumulated 43 steals, while Victor Hithe and Craig Biggio had 31 apiece. The 1987 team also dominated in Asheville, losing only three home games during June, July and August.

Mike Simms, who paced the league's first basemen with 1,069 putouts and 1,158 chances, kept the baserunners moving by establishing a league and Asheville franchise record with 39 home runs. His partner in power was South Atlantic League Most Valuable Player Ed Whited, who led the circuit with a .323 batting average and 126 RBIs while ranking second to Simms with 28 home runs.

The Astros also sent Craig Biggio, the twenty-second player taken overall in the 1987 draft, to Asheville after selecting him out of Seton Hall University. A catcher while with the Tourists, Biggio looked every bit the top prospect while hitting .375 with 9 home runs, 49 RBIs and 31 stolen bases in 64 games. In the *Asheville Citizen-Times*, Jim Baker described Biggio's contributions thus: "Biggio hit second in the batting order, filled the gaps with line drives, stole bases, choreographed a talented pitching staff and muddied his uniform every night."

After back-to-back ninety-win seasons, the Tourists experienced some turmoil in 1988. Manager Gary Tuck resigned on May 18 after the team got off to a 16–23 start. Jim Coveney, a junior college coach from Arizona who was slated to manage Houston's New York–Penn League club, did a laudable job in a difficult situation to lead Asheville to an overall mark of 65–75.

Other disturbances included center fielder Ramon Cedeno, a .315 hitter whose season came to an early end on July 10 when he discovered how little give the dugout walls at Greensboro's War Memorial Stadium had after he stuck out and punched one of them. Fellow outfielder Dan Nyssen, a .284 hitter, decided to quit the game after being sent to Asheville from the Florida State League on May 18. He returned to the Tourists a day after Cedeno's boxing exhibition and manned the middle garden for the remainder of the slate.

There were high points to the campaign, headlined by Eric Anthony's minor league–leading 29 home runs. Anthony even missed the first month of the campaign after injuring an ankle on the first day of spring training. He batted a modest .273 with the Tourists, yet led the South Atlantic League with 37 doubles and a .560 slugging percentage and was the Tourists' lone representative in the SAL All-Star Game. He also set the league record with 66 extra-base hits.

Blaise Ilsley was named the South Atlantic League Pitcher of the Year in 1986 even though he was promoted to the Florida State League at midseason. *Author's collection.*

BLAISE ILSLEY
Ashville   P

Third baseman Ed Whited led the South Atlantic League with a .323 batting average and 126 RBIs to outdistance teammate Mike Simms for the circuit's Most Valuable Player award in 1987. *Author's collection.*

Dean Hartgraves struck out eleven Myrtle Beach batters during a seven-inning no-hitter in 1988. *Author's collection.*

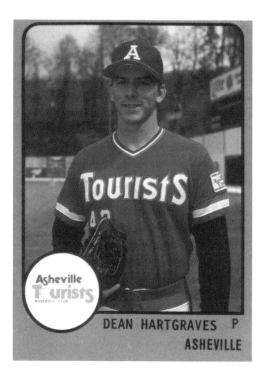

Outfielder Willie Ansley earned national acclaim after hitting .309 with 55 RBIs and 53 stolen bases with Asheville prior to a midseason promotion in 1989. *Author's collection.*

The other highlight took place on August 12, 1988. In the second game of a doubleheader against the Myrtle Beach Blue Jays, southpaw Dean Hartgraves fired a seven-inning no-hitter while fanning eleven batters and walking two. Six days earlier, teammate Mike Hook took a no-hitter into the ninth inning against the Charleston Rainbows, only to settle for his third of four two-hitters after surrendering a safety with one out in the final frame.

Asheville's log of future Major Leaguers increased during the final three weeks of the 1989 season when Kenny Lofton was promoted after spending most of the campaign in the New York–Penn League. The speedy Lofton made his Tourists debut on August 21, 1989, and stroked a line drive home run in his first plate appearance at McCormick Field. He proceeded to steal three bases and score three times in the first five innings of that contest, and by the end of the season had hit .329 with fourteen swipes in eighty-two at-bats.

"[Manager] Jim [Coveney] worked with me to stay over the ball and keep my swing level to make contact," Lofton told Chris Smith. "That helped me keep the ball on the ground, where I could use my speed to reach base. Those mechanics I learned in Asheville helped me throughout my career."

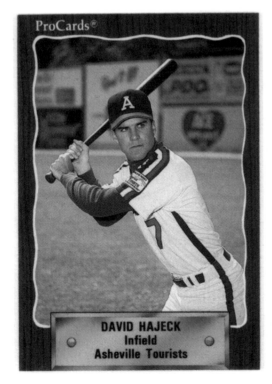

Infielder Dave Hajek was a non-drafted free agent who earned league all-star honors in 1990. Hajek returned to Asheville in 2004 as the Tourists' batting coach. *Author's collection*.

A History of Professional Baseball in *Asheville*

Earlier in 1989, Willie Ansley swiped bags like a thief and earned a spot in the SAL All-Star Game prior to his promotion to Double-A Columbus. Possessing both speed and power, Ansley hit .309 with 6 home runs, 55 RBIs and 53 stolen bases in 340 at-bats for the Tourists. Shortstop Andujar Cedeno made significant strides with the leather by cutting his errors in half during the second half of the campaign while coming through with numerous multi-hit efforts. Thirteen rainouts kept attendance down to 96,178, which led to the installation of another drainage system in the infield along with a new brand of infield dirt, known as Pave Rouge.

The 1990 Tourists were again also-rans in the South Atlantic League, finishing in last place during the first half before contending in August for the second half crown. Dave Hajek, who would coach in Asheville for two-and-a-half years from 2004 to 2006, had a remarkable professional debut. In addition to earning all-star recognition, the non-drafted infielder from Cal Poly Pomona earned a pair of South Atlantic League Batter of the Week accolades, hitting .529 in ten games at the start of the season before posting sixteen hits in thirty-one trips to the plate while scoring twelve times in a seven-game stretch in July. Shortstop Orlando Miller joined Hajek as a starter in the SAL All-Star Game, while center fielder Brian Hunter blossomed into a Major League–caliber performer after moving from the lower third of the batting order to the leadoff spot.

Eighth Inning

*B*y the late 1980s, McCormick Field was showing its age. General manager Ron McKee said the wooden structure was held together only by the countless coats of paint that had been applied over the past six decades. Yet the feel generated by the ballpark led to its fifteen seconds of fame in *Bull Durham*. According to the movie's co-producer, Mark Burg, Asheville was selected for the two-day shoot on October 5–6, 1987, "because of its look and because the director saw the park and fell in love with it."

The movie's story is centered on two players, veteran catcher Crash Davis (Kevin Costner) and up-and-coming pitcher Nook LaLoosh (Tim Robbins), whose careers become intertwined with that of a "baseball annie," Annie Savoy (Susan Sarandon). While Nook reaches the Major Leagues toward the end of the movie, Crash receives his release and signs with the Tourists. Crash is shown driving up to McCormick Field prior to breaking the minor league home run record. The ball disappears in the trees and bushes over the left-field wall, and the third-base coach greets Crash while he rounds the bases and hears the cheers of a modest crowd nestled in the old blue wooden bleachers.

Yes, the ballpark had its charms, but after sixty-eight years of service, a leaking roof and an unstable floor that saw one sportswriter step through a rotten board were signs as subtle as a sledgehammer that a replacement was needed.

With that in mind, the Buncombe County commissioners worked with the architectural firm Bowers, Ellis, and Watson along with the Tourists to design a new McCormick Field on the same location. The blue wooden grandstand

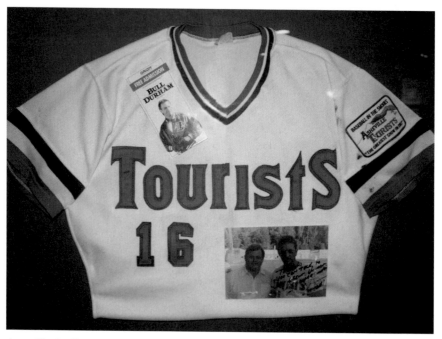

Actor Kevin Costner wore an Asheville Tourists uniform toward the end of the movie *Bull Durham*. A portion of the movie was filmed for two days in Asheville in 1987. *Ron McKee collection.*

McCormick Field was nearing its end when this postcard photograph was taken in March of 1988. *Author's collection.*

with its metal folding chairs for box seats and view-blocking posts gave way to 3,500 permanent seats with supposed room for expansion between the final pitch of the 1991 season and the first home game of the 1992 slate. After cutting a few corners on various expenditures, the county footed the $3-million bill, with Leader Construction Company serving as the general contractor. The diamond remained the same, as did the layout of the seats, with the new structure providing fans with expanded restrooms, modern concession stands, a plaza for group outings and a new clubhouse for the Tourists.

The original McCormick Field went out with a bang September 1, 1991. Unfortunately, it was the roar of thunder that closed the history books on the minor leagues' oldest stadium. Al Harley's routine fly ball to left field in the bottom of the eighth inning preceded the pouring rains, which forced the premature ending and gave Gastonia an 11–5 victory over the Tourists.

"There's mixed emotions," Ron McKee said just prior to the final game. "You think with your heart and you think with your head. In your heart there's a lot of sentimentality, because I feel like I grew up here. But it's going to be so much nicer for the fans and we'll have a little more room for offices. This year we've had people working in storage closets."

The 1991 Tourists were one of the youngest clubs in the minor leagues, averaging nineteen years of age and one season of professional experience. The team struggled to post a 55–83 record, yet managed to set the South Atlantic League standard for most runs scored in a shutout during a 20–0 rout over Gastonia in August. Some 117,628 fans entered McCormick Field in its final campaign, a total that represented the third largest in franchise history. The ballpark's finale also attracted attention from throughout the United States, with reporters from such national publications as *Baseball America*, *Sports Illustrated* and *Baseball Weekly* descending upon Asheville to say good-bye.

"This stadium is everything you picture minor league baseball being," Tom Nevers, Houston's 1990 first-round draft pick, said prior to the game. "I told some friends that I want to hit the last home run ever hit here. When you think of all the great people that have played on this field before us, it's kind of neat being a part of history."

Nevers accomplished his goal when he clubbed a three-run homer over the right-field wall in the third inning. A couple of hours later as the skies cleared, The Byrds played "Turn, Turn, Turn" during a postgame concert and McCormick Field handed its reins as the oldest minor league ballpark to Spartanburg's Duncan Park.

"It's a happy day, yet a sad day," said Tourists batting coach Bob Robertson, who played for Asheville in 1966. "There's so much history and heritage here that it's an honor for me to work on the same field as guys like Ruth and Gehrig. But it's also sad because that part of history is leaving here."

Tom Nevers told the author prior to the final game at McCormick Field that he wanted to hit the last home run at the ballpark. His wish came true against the Gastonia Rangers. *Author's collection.*

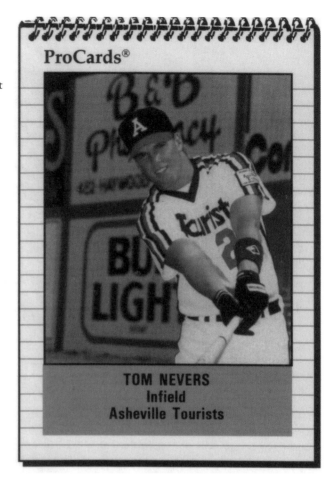

ProCards®

TOM NEVERS
Infield
Asheville Tourists

The changes in Asheville coincided with the Tourists receiving the 1991 Bob Freitas Award among Class A teams. Considered by many as the minor leagues' equivalent to an Oscar in the motion picture industry, the Freitas Award recognized the McKees' dedication to building the Tourists from a debt-ridden franchise to one of professional baseball's crown jewels. Upon accepting the award, Ron McKee looked toward the future, stating, "This new ballpark was desperately needed and the citizens of the city and the county had the great foresight to see it. I also want to say that the new park is not for the team. It's for the public and I hope they bring their families just as they and their parents were brought here as children to experience the magic of the ballpark and the other things that go along with it."

The new McCormick Field hosted its first game on April 17, 1992, with the Tourists dropping a 3–0 decision to the Spartanburg Phillies. A crowd

A ticket for the final game of the old McCormick Field in 1991 and a ticket from the first game at the new McCormick Field in 1992. *Ron McKee collection.*

of 4,116 watched the proceedings, with nearly a thousand turned away at the gates. A day later, Asheville's Eduardo Ramos hit the first home run at McCormick Field. When Ron McKee told Ramos he had joined a legacy that included the likes of Tom Nevers and Willie Stargell, Ramos said, "I know who Tom Nevers is, but who's Willie Stargell?"

More than 119,000 fans clicked the turnstiles during the ballpark's rebirth, and much of their cheers were aimed toward an eighteen-year-old Venezuelan whose name few knew how to pronounce correctly. One of Bobby Abreu's most poignant minor league memories stems from his first full professional season as a member of the Tourists. Every time he stepped to the plate, the public address announcer yelled his name as "Bobby Ab-ROOOOOO!" Problem was, Abreu's name is pronounced "a-BRAY-u," only his shyness and inability to speak English prevented him from telling anyone until the last week of the season. That had little affect on his performance on the field, for

A History of Professional Baseball in *Asheville*

Abreu hit .292 and ranked among the Astros' organizational leaders with 81 runs, 140 hits and 63 walks while registering 15 assists from right field.

The 1993 Tourists sent four players to the South Atlantic League All-Star Game. While Sean Fesh, who led the league with 65 appearances and topped the Tourists with 20 saves and 10 wins, and Greg Elliott, with 11 home runs, 25 doubles and 55 RBIs, proved to be little more than footnotes in baseball history, Richard Hidalgo and Melvin Mora were established Major Leaguers by the end of the decade. Mora placed second on the Tourists with a .285 batting average. Hidalgo, who was a relative baby at the start of the season as a seventeen-year-old, batted at a .270 clip with 10 home runs and 55 RBIs while displaying deceptive speed and an arm with shotgun strength from right field.

The Tourists introduced a new logo in 1994, featuring a Hawaiian shirt-clad bear with a bat over his right shoulder and a suitcase in his left hand, designed by Steve Millard. That same year Asheville began its relationship with the expansion Colorado Rockies. Again, the change in affiliation did nothing to alter the Tourists' hard-hitting reputation, even with the 1992 addition of the 35-foot wall in right field to help equalize the short distance of 301 feet. At the time it was the second-highest wall in professional baseball, only two feet shorter than Fenway Park's Green Monster.

The first Rockies-affiliated Tourists team led the South Atlantic League with 122 home runs behind former University of Michigan linebacker Nate Holdren, who overcame a dismal first half to tie Greensboro's Ruben Rivera for the league crown with 28 round-trippers. Doug Walls struck out 111 batters in 106⅓ innings, including 14 in one game, and John Thomson registered a 2.85 ERA in 19 outings while going 6–6. Jamey Wright posted a mediocre 7–14 mark but showed impressive poise and competitiveness to become in 1996 the first Tourists player under the Rockies' affiliation to reach the big leagues. Local product Darren Holmes also made an appearance while rehabbing a sore right elbow. A native of nearby Fletcher and a graduate of T.C. Roberson High School, Holmes whiffed seven and allowed only one hit in three innings before a sold-out crowd at McCormick Field.

Given McCormick Field's reputation as a hitter's haven, the 1995 Tourists did what most observers thought impossible. Under the guidance of pitching coach Jack Lamabe, the Asheville staff tied for first in the South Atlantic League with a 3.14 ERA and ranked second on the circuit with thirteen shutouts. Equally odd were the performers, a pair of Canadians drafted in 1994 who earned all-star recognition. Michael Kusiewicz paced the Class A league with a 2.06 ERA, a norm aided by allowing only thirty-four walks during the campaign. Brent Crowther had a 2.28 ERA, twelve wins in fifteen starts, and led the SAL with three complete games.

First baseman Todd Helton received significant attention in Asheville after the former University of Tennessee two-way standout was sent to the Tourists when the Colorado Rockies made him their first-round draft pick in 1995. *Asheville Tourists.*

Asheville's offense was far from formidable aside from the efforts of outfielder Derrick Gibson. The former football standout paced all minor leaguers with 115 RBIs to go with 148 hits, 91 runs, 32 home runs, 10 triples and a .533 slugging percentage. He also stole 31 bases, making him the first 30–30 player in the minor leagues since 1987.

The 1995 season also brought to Asheville first baseman Todd Helton. Selected in the first round of the June draft, Helton was a two-sport star at the University of Tennessee who hit a modest .254 in 200 at-bats with the Tourists. Noticeably exhausted after his collegiate tenure that included a trip to the College World Series, Helton showed little of the power (1 home run and 15 RBIs) he would soon display in the Major Leagues. His presence, however, did provide a spark for the Tourists, who wound up winning nine of their last ten regular season games to capture the North Division in the second half before losing to the Piedmont Phillies in the first round of the playoffs.

In 1996 the Tourists jumped out to a 26–6 start and won the first half with a 47–20 record, tops in the minor leagues. The club finished the slate with an 84–52 mark before ousting Columbia in a three-game series in the first round of the playoffs. Heavy rain in Asheville forced the second round to be played entirely at Delmarva, with the Shorebirds winning two of the three contests against the Tourists.

Scott Randall gave the Tourists a shot at winning every time he took the mound that season. Possessing excellent command and a knee-bending curveball, "Randy" won his first six decisions and became the season's first minor leaguer to reach the ten-win mark. He also threw a pair of no-hitters, the first coming on July 17, 1996, when he became only the fourth Asheville hurler to toss a no-no in a nine-inning contest. His other gem was an eleven-inning, eleven-strikeout performance that earned him nothing more than a no-decision. The Tourists defeated Augusta, 2–1, in nineteen innings, which represented the longest game in the minors that season.

Catcher Ben Petrick, Colorado's second-round draft pick from the previous June, handled the catching chores in 1996 and batted .235 with 14 home runs, 19 stolen bases and 52 RBIs to earn a spot on *Baseball America*'s postseason Class A all-star team. He climbed to Coors Field in 1999 and played parts of five seasons in the Major Leagues, prior to retiring in 2003 due to complications from Parkinson's disease.

Jake Westbrook lived up to his reputation as a first-round draft pick by posting an Asheville team-high 14 wins in 1997. *Author's collection.*

Juan Pierre emerged as a prototype center fielder and leadoff hitter while toiling for the Tourists in 1999. *Asheville Tourists.*

More than 145,000 fans entered McCormick Field to set a Tourists' franchise attendance record in 1996. The Tourists also hosted the South Atlantic League All-Star Game that saw the North defeat the South, 4–3, in front of nearly 4,500 fans. The ballpark also welcomed the Silver Bullets, a traveling women's professional baseball team managed by Hall of Fame pitcher Phil Niekro.

The 1997 season was uneventful from a wins-and-losses standpoint under manager Ron Gideon, yet featured first-round draft pick Jake Westbrook and third-rounder Shawn Chacon. Westbrook, a Georgia native, led the Tourists in wins with a 14–11 record and a 4.29 ERA in 28 games. Chacon, who reeled off a league-best 10 straight victories before dropping his last two decisions, posted an 11–7 mark and led the Asheville rotation with 149 strikeouts and a 3.89 ERA.

"I have great memories of pitching in Asheville," said Chacon, who concluded the 2006 season with the Pittsburgh Pirates. "It was my first real season in pro ball and I was part of a good pitching staff where everyone challenged each other. Asheville reminded me a lot of Colorado, and the fans there were great. I felt like I got off to a good start in my career there."

A History of Professional Baseball in *Asheville*

The Tourists were also-rans in 1998 while finishing two games above the .500 mark. Josh Kalinowski went 12–10 with a 3.92 ERA and led the minor leagues with 215 strikeouts in 172⅓ innings of work. In 1999 an unheralded twelfth-round draft pick out of the University of South Alabama, outfielder Juan Pierre, displayed one of the most impressive work ethics ever witnessed at McCormick Field. His efforts resulted in a .320 batting average while leading the South Atlantic League with 187 hits, 585 at-bats and 140 games played. Despite ranking among the league leaders throughout the campaign, Pierre was bypassed for the SAL All-Star Game. Pierre took the news in stride.

"When I was in A ball, I was not a real big prospect," said Pierre, who reached the Rockies in 2001. "I had to work hard and prove myself every time I took the field. I knew that was the only opportunity that I would have and I was determined to make the most of it. But the big leagues still felt like they were a million miles away."

Midway through the 1999 slate, the Tourists received Jason Jennings, who earlier in the year had been named *Baseball America*'s College Player of the Year while attending Baylor University. Jennings made 12 starts with the Tourists shortly after he was the Rockies' first-round draft choice. The right-hander had a 2–2 record and a 3.70 ERA, including 69 strikeouts in 58⅓ innings with Asheville.

Another standout in 1999 was shortstop Juan Uribe. Two years removed from signing out of the Dominican Republic, Uribe batted .267 with 9 home runs and 46 RBIs and registered a 15-game hitting streak with the Tourists. Two years later he got the nod in Colorado. Uribe was later traded to the Chicago White Sox, where he won the world championship in 2005 after making a spectacular catch on a foul ball down the left-field line in the ninth inning of the fourth and final game.

Ninth Inning

I f the latter half of the 1920s was the "Struttin' Bud" Shaney era in Asheville, the current decade will prove to be the Joe Mikulik era at McCormick Field. After fifteen seasons in the professional ranks, Mikulik's career in 2000 was back where it started, in Asheville. In 1985, his first full season as a player, the Texas native had his best all-around campaign by leading the Tourists with 141 hits and 14 game-winning RBIs. He also earned South Atlantic League all-star honors while batting .267 with 23 home runs and 87 RBIs.

It was during his season with Asheville that Mikulik met his wife, Kathy. The couple married after the 1985 campaign and moved to nearby Candler in 1992, just prior to the end of his playing days. After turning his efforts to coaching in 1995, Mikulik was offered the Asheville job by the Rockies for the 2000 season.

"It was strange," Mikulik said of his first season. "There were a few times when I was sitting on the bench and I'd catch myself going back in time. I remember grabbing a bat and wanting nothing more than to drive a ball out of McCormick Field. I came out to the ballpark over the offseason and looked around and wondered where all those years went. It seems like yesterday when I was playing here, but now I couldn't ask for a better situation."

The results proved the man known as Mik was indeed a perfect fit. No Tourists manager has ever guided the team for seven straight seasons as Mikulik had through the 2006 campaign. He also ranked second in career victories among Asheville skippers, just a few notches behind Ray Hathaway's franchise-leading total of 518, which Mik is projected to surpass during the early stages of 2007.

A History of Professional Baseball in *Asheville*

With his fiery personality and aggressive approach to the game, Mikulik's popularity was never a question in Asheville, but his notoriety increased on the national level following the events of June 25, 2006, in Lexington. Mikulik earned an overnight reputation as one of the minors' premier debaters during the course of arguing a call on a pickoff attempt at second base. In the process of proving his point, Mikulik demonstrated how to dive back into the bag, call a strike, kick dirt on an umpire's feet, spike a water bottle at home plate and throw a base, resin bag and a multitude of bats. The showing earned him a $1,000 fine and a seven-day suspension from the South Atlantic League as well as several days' worth of highlights on television stations across the country.

The Tourists' front office received nearly one thousand responses from fans, many of whom were expressing their dismay over Mikulik's behavior and the example it set. Others raved about the memories of Earl Weaver, Billy Martin, Lou Piniella, et al., and the lost art of arguing with an umpire.

During the subsequent media frenzy, Tourists assistant general manager Chris Smith obtained the base from the Legends in hopes of auctioning it for charity. The results exceeded even Smith's expectations when $5,000 was raised. Tom McGowan, a fan visiting Asheville from Philadelphia, won the base and donated it back, which is what the second-place finisher, Craig Boyce, did as well. The base wound up going to Mark Sturnell, operator of Hannah Flanagan's restaurant, where the bag autographed by Mikulik now resides. As a result, the Asheville Tourists Children's Fund, which provides shoes for needy children throughout Western North Carolina, received $4,050 from the auction, and a Lexington charity garnered $850 of the proceeds.

"The response, both to Mik's tirade and the auction, was unbelievable," said Smith. "In many ways it was a perfect storm. But when you look at the money that was raised, this story definitely had a happy ending."

As manager, Mikulik's rosters have contained numerous players with promise. In Mikulik's first season as the Asheville skipper, Tourists fans poured into McCormick Field and set an annual attendance mark of 162,395. While the team's 66–69 record was not spectacular, there were some impressive pitching performances, led by Taiwanese right-hander Chin-hui Tsao. The eighteen-year-old Tsao, who received a Colorado-record $2.2-million signing bonus, was among the minor league leaders with 187 strikeouts while posting an 11–8 record and a 2.73 ERA in 24 starts. Aaron Cook returned to Asheville in 2000 and won 10 games while ranking seventh in the league with a 2.97 ERA. Julio DePaula won 8 games and tossed a no-hitter while fanning 12 Cape Fear batters in a 1–0 victory over the Crocs on June 26.

The 2001 Tourists went from worst to first, finishing in last place in the South Atlantic League's South Division with a 27–43 record in the first half before rebounding to go 41–28 in the second stanza to end up two games

Joe Mikulik earned the admiration of Asheville fans with his fiery approach as manager of the Tourists, beginning in 2000. Mikulik once threw a toilet on the field after being tossed from a game by an umpire. *Photograph by Tony Farlow.*

Joe Mikulik poses with the base he threw in Lexington in 2006. The incident earned Mikulik a $1,000 fine and a seven-day suspension, but it also raised nearly $5,000 for the Asheville Tourists Children's Fund. *Photograph by Tony Farlow.*

ahead of Columbus. The Tourists ousted Augusta in the first round of the playoffs to advance to the championship series. Asheville lost the first two games at Lexington before play came to a halt following the tragic events of September 11.

Joe Mikulik was named the SAL 2001 Manager of the Year and outfielder–first baseman Rene Reyes was tabbed the loop's Most Valuable Player. Reyes hit a league-leading .322 with 11 home runs and 61 RBIs while stealing 53 bases and ranking second on the circuit with 156 hits. Outfielder Brad Hawpe hit .267 with a team-high 22 home runs and 72 RBIs and shortstop Clint Barmes batted .260 with 5 home runs and 24 RBIs in 74 games. Both Hawpe and Barmes emerged as solid contributors in Colorado during the 2005 season. On the mound, Scott Dohmann went 11–13 with a 4.32 ERA and nearly tasted perfection with a one-hitter at Charleston on July 29.

Another Tourist-turned-Rockie was pitcher Jeff Francis, who joined Asheville after being drafted in the first round in 2002. Francis posted a 1.80 ERA in four starts before suffering a concussion after being struck in the side of the head with a foul ball while watching a game in the McCormick Field home dugout. Francis's career took off in 2004 when he was named the Minor League Player of the Year by going a combined 16–3 between stints at the Double-A and Triple-A levels.

Jeff Salazar posted Most Valuable Player–caliber numbers for the Tourists in 2003 while playing stellar defense in center field. *Author's collection.*

Asheville put together a decent won-lost record in 2003 by going 74–65, yet tied for third in the South Division. Much of the team's success was generated by center fielder Jeff Salazar, who made countless spectacular plays in the middle garden while clubbing opponents from the middle of the order. A product of Oklahoma State University, Salazar led the league with 109 runs, 29 homers and 98 RBIs, contributed 28 stolen bases and batted at a .284 clip. At the end of the slate, Salazar was named to the TOPPS Class A all-star team, but the fact he was not selected as the league's Most Valuable Player was a travesty of justice in the eyes of most Tourists fans.

In 2004 third baseman Ian Stewart put together an effort that left many longtime Asheville fans believing his performance ranked among the all-time best. Drafted by the Colorado Rockies in the first round in 2003, Stewart thrilled the patrons with his spectacular defense and all-out hustle. The ball popped off his bat like grease from a frying pan, producing a league-leading 300 total bases, 70 extra-base hits and a .594 slugging percentage while placing second on the circuit with 30 homers and 161 hits. His shaggy hair, friendly demeanor with kids and willingness to sign autographs until everyone had received one left the McCormick Field faithful feeling fortunate to have had such a positive influence come through town. Those beliefs also were held by Joe Mikulik, who saw his daughter, Susan, marry Stewart in Asheville in 2006.

In 2005 first baseman Joe Koshansky, a strapping left-handed slugger from the University of Virginia, swatted a league-best 36 home runs while with the Tourists and hit two more following an August 23 promotion to Double-A Tulsa to rank second in the minors in round-trippers. Yet, when the statistics revealed that Koshansky batted .355 with 25 homers in 61 games at McCormick Field compared to a .227 norm with 11 homers in 59 road outings in the South Atlantic League, most observers added the first baseman's name to the list that includes Richard Johnson. Koshansky, however, silenced those critics when he posted an encore performance at Tulsa in 2006 and was selected to play in the Futures All-Star Game.

"I heard it a lot that the only reason I had so many home runs was because of the short porch in Asheville," Koshansky said. "I was always confident that I could play at any level, but it is nice to put up some numbers again. It's hard not to hear things when everyone is writing and saying things, and the last thing you want to have happen is to let those things get in your head."

Koshansky provided a dangerous one-two punch in the middle of the Asheville lineup with left fielder Matt Miller. Miller was named the South Atlantic League's Most Valuable Player in 2005 after pacing the circuit with 168 hits and 292 total bases while tying for second with a .331 batting average. He also contributed 30 home runs and 100 RBIs, making Miller and Koshansky the first set of Tourists teammates to produce 30-homer efforts in the same season.

A History of Professional Baseball in *Asheville*

First-round draft pick Ian Stewart thrilled Asheville fans with his potent bat and all-out hustle on defense at third base. *Photograph by Tony Farlow.*

First baseman Joe Koshansky pounded South Atlantic League pitchers for 25 home runs in 61 games at McCormick Field in 2005. *Photograph by Tony Farlow.*

Asheville Tourists President Ron McKee and Palace Sports & Entertainment Vice-president Sean Henry discuss the team's sale at a press conference in August 2005. *Photograph by Tony Farlow.*

Asheville was represented by a league-high five players at the 2006 South Atlantic League All-Star Game. *From left to right*, Eric Young Jr., Brandon Durden, Dexter Fowler, David Patton and Chris Nelson. *Author's collection.*

A History of Professional Baseball in *Asheville*

Just prior to Joe Koshansky's promotion to Tulsa, the most significant move in recent Tourists history occurred on August 12, 2005, when Palace Sports & Entertainment purchased the team from Woody Kern and Ron McKee, effective October 1, for $6 million. Unlike the old-school operation of the McKees, PS&E entered the South Atlantic League as a major player in the world of professional sports. In addition to the Tourists, the company headed by Bill Davidson also owned the 2004 Stanley Cup Champion Tampa Bay Lightning, the NBA's Detroit Pistons, the WNBA's Detroit Shock, The Palace of Auburn Hills and three outdoor amphitheaters.

"We are thrilled with the opportunity to own and operate the Asheville Tourists," said Ron Campbell, executive vice-president of Palace Sports & Entertainment. "Our intentions are to maintain, further develop and operate a first-class organization in Asheville, one that the entire community will continue to be proud to call its own. Creating a premier fan experience is at the core of our business practice."

PS&E initiated a variety of upgrades that gave McCormick Field many of the modern conveniences fans had come to expect in the minor leagues over the past decade. The changes began in late January by tearing down the outfield wall and replacing it with a Major League–style wall along with a video scoreboard three times the size of the previous one. Other additions included a new picnic area down the left-field line and an upscale club seating area for sixty season ticket holders. New box seats also were installed in May. Working with the City of Asheville, PS&E invested more than $700,000 into the ballpark upgrades.

"We're doing everything possible to improve the amenities for our fans while preserving the history that has taken place at the ballpark," said Tourists executive director Mike Bauer. "This is the first wave of several things we want to do to make McCormick Field one of the premier venues in the minor leagues for years to come."

The changes led to a new season record in attendance, with nearly 170,000 fans visiting McCormick Field in 2006. On the field, second baseman Eric Young Jr. established the franchise's single-season stolen base record when he swiped his eighty-second bag on August 27. Young joined teammates Dexter Fowler, Chris Young, Brandon Durden and David Patton as Asheville's representatives at the South Atlantic League All-Star Game in Eastlake, Ohio, on June 20.

More changes are sure to take place on the Asheville baseball scene in the coming years. While there has been talk in years past of building a modern facility with plenty of parking, possibly along Airport Road, Palace Sports continues to make McCormick Field a viable venue for the quintessential minor league baseball experience. Either way, if the Tourists' past in any way proves to be a harbinger of things to come, baseball in Asheville should continue to thrive as "The Greatest Show on Dirt."

Bibliography

Asheville Chamber of Commerce. *Live and Invest in the Land of the Sky*, 1926.

Asheville Citizen.

Asheville Citizen-Times.

Asheville Daily Citizen.

Asheville Gazette-News.

Asheville Times.

Asheville Tourists programs and scorecards, 1968–2005.

Ballew, Bill. *Baseball In Asheville*. Charleston, SC: Arcadia Publishing, 2004.

Creamer, Robert W. *Babe: The Legend Comes To Life*. New York: Simon & Schuster, 1974.

Johnson, Lloyd, and Miles Wolff. *The Encyclopedia of Minor League Baseball*. 2nd edition. Durham, NC: Baseball America, 1997.

Terrell, Bob. *The Old Ball Yard: McCormick Field Home of Memories*. Alexander, NC: WorldComm, 1997.

Utley, R.G. (Hank), and Scott Verner. *The Independent Carolina Baseball League, 1936–38*. Jefferson, NC: McFarland & Company, 1999.

About the Author

*B*ill Ballew is a freelance baseball writer and the author of seven previous books. A 1983 graduate of the University of Georgia's Grady School of Journalism, he has served as the part-time media relations director for the Asheville Tourists since 2002. The Hickory, North Carolina native spends countless evenings coaching his twelve-year-old son, Brad, and nine-year-old son, Bryce, in baseball. He and his wife, Hope, reside in Arden. To contact Bill, go to www.baseballbill.net.